Linking Up

Planning Your Traffic-Free Bike Trip between

Pittsburgh PA and Washington DC

via the Great Allegheny Passage

and the C & O Canal Towpath

http:// yockatomac.org

Mary Shaw and **Roy Weil**

with lots of help from

Other Folks Who've Made the Trip

Third Edition, Summer 2007

Proceeds support trail development

Credits

Printed in United States of America

ISBN 978-0-9792108-1-5

Published by Great Allegheny Press, c/o Regional Trail Corporation, PO Box 95, West Newton PA 15089

Third edition 3 2 1

The online version is available at http://yockatomac.org/linkup/ We will be delighted if you refer to this material from your web pages by linking to ours, but you may not copy our content to your own pages.

Acknowledgements

Thanks to all the people who have made the long ride with us and to those who have offered suggestions about this guide. Thanks also to all the volunteers who develop and maintain the trails and to Sandra Finley and Michele Gornick, with Allegheny Trail Alliance, for assistance in updating our database of services.

Contents

On Safety, Judgment, and Personal Responsibility

We compiled this information to support individual trail users and the development of the trail systems. We have made a diligent effort to present accurate descriptions and to confirm trail conditions and services. However, we are human, trails change with time, and we occasionally receive incorrect information. Weather, wear, construction, vandalism, changes in land status, and other forces can alter conditions, erode trail surfaces, create obstacles, or even close trails. Businesses can close or change management, and quality may change as a result. Therefore we cannot be responsible for discrepancies between these descriptions and actual conditions. If you do encounter any discrepancies, please let us know.

Trail activities have intrinsic risks, for which you must assume responsibility; we cannot be responsible for mishaps or problems you encounter on your trip. Everyone who sets out on a trip assumes personal responsibility for his or her own safety as well as the safety of others on the trip. Ultimately the quality of your experience depends on your own common sense and good judgment.

Emergency Contacts

Occasionally something goes wrong, and you need to call for help. The standard emergency number in all areas along these trails is 911.

Cellular phone coverage is spotty along the trails. Nevertheless, if you have a cellular phone you might want to carry it in case of emergency. Your emergency might happen to take place in an area that does have service.

If you can find a willing friend who's not joining you on the trip, give everyone that person's telephone number as a message drop. If anyone who gets separated from the group and needs help can leave a message at this number. When the group notices that someone's missing, they can call this number and ask for messages. If you do this with a fancy voicemail system or answering machine, be sure everyone knows how to use it.

Introduction

So you're thinking about a bike ride between Pittsburgh PA and Washington DC, and you don't want to ride in traffic? That's great! The C&O Canal Towpath has long been a favorite route, especially nice for bicycle camping. Now that the Towpath is connected Pittsburgh PA via the rail-trails of the Great Allegheny Passage, the route is even better.

We begin with answers to the questions that people most often ask when they start to think about the trip, followed by suggestions about things to plan for and ideas about itineraries. At the end, we list services and amenities you may find helpful and give a table of distances between towns. With few exceptions, we include all the services we know about (mid 2007) that are within reasonable cycling distance of the trail. If you have a support car you can range farther afield, but other guides provide better coverage of those larger areas than we can possibly hope to.

For up-to-date information on services and facilities along the trail, check the Allegheny Trail Alliance web site at http://www.ATATrail.org. For additional planning resources, visit http://www.yockatomac.org .

To get another copy of this book – say, to give to a friend or to have one of your own after you return a borrowed copy – send email to ATAmail@atatrail.org or call the Allegheny Trail Alliance office toll-free at 888-ATA-BIKE.

The Great Allegheny Passage

The Great Allegheny Passage links Cumberland MD to Pittsburgh PA on rail-trails, with a spur to the Pittsburgh Airport via the Montour Trail. Several trail groups develop and maintain sections of the Passage: Allegheny Highlands Trails Maryland, Somerset County Rails to Trails Association, Regional Trail Corporation, Steel Valley Trail Council, and Friends of the Riverfront.

Recent (2006) trail construction has completed the Great Allegheny Passage between Washington DC and Cumberland MD, you will now find a complete trail between DC and McKeesport.

Trail Name Abbreviations Used in this Guide

Trails of the Great Allegheny Passage

GAP	Great Allegheny Passage
ATA	Allegheny Trail Alliance
YRTS	Youghiogheny River Trail South
YRTN	Youghiogheny River Trail North
SVT	Steel Valley Trail
TRHT	Three Rivers Heritage Trail
MnTr	Montour Trail
AHT	Allegheny Highlands Trail

Other Trails

C & O Canal Towpath	
WMRT	Western Maryland Rail Trail
CapCr	Capital Crescent Trail
MtVer	Mount Vernon Trail
4MiRn	Four Mile Run Trail
W&OD	Washington & Old Dominion Trail
AndBW	Anderson Bikeway

Frequently Asked Questions

We have ridden the entire trip from DC to Pittsburgh on these trails nine times, and we've ridden most sections many times on shorter trips. In the process, we learned a lot about the route. People often ask us about planning similar trips. You may also be interested in our answers.

Is the trail finished?

Almost. There are (in mid 2007) one unfinished section, one seasonal detour, and one permanent detour between Pittsburgh PA and Washington DC. We tell you about them on p. 16.

Where does the trail go? How long is it?

The trail connects Pittsburgh PA to Washington DC. It runs on the rail-trails of the Great Allegheny Passage from Pittsburgh to Cumberland MD, then down the C&O Canal Towpath to Washington. Eventually the Montour and Steel Valley Trails will add connections to Pittsburgh and the Airport. Here are the trails, with lengths and locations of open sections and detours.

	Distance		*Trail Route*			*Unfinished*
Section	*Open*	*Detour*	*From*	*Via*	*To*	*Portion*
Three Rivers Heritage Trail (TRHT)	3 mi	3 mi	Pittsburgh PA	Hazelwood PA	Glenwood Bridge PA	Hazelwood-Glenwood Br
Steel Valley Trail (SVT)	1 mi	10 mi	Glenwood Bridge PA	Duquesne PA	McKeesport PA	Glenwood Br-McKeesport
Youghiogheny River Trail North (YRTN)	44 mi	none	McKeesport PA	West Newton PA	Connellsville PA	none
Youghiogheny River Trail South (YRTS)	27 mi	none	Connellsville PA	Ohiopyle PA	Confluence PA	none
Allegheny Highlands Trail in Pa (AHTPa)	42 mi	11 mi in winter	Confluence PA	Meyersdale PA	PA-MD state line	Winter tunnel detour (p. 16)
Allegheny Highlands Trail in Md (AHTMd)	20 mi	none	PA-MD state line	Frostburg MD	Cumberland MD	none
C&O Canal Towpath (C&O)	182 mi	4 mi	Cumberland MD	Williamsport MD	Washington DC	Road detour near Dam 4

The total distance Washington, DC to Pittsburgh is about 319 miles on trails and 16 trail miles that still require road detours (we discuss detours on p. 16).

Can I make this trip on my road bike? How about my hybrid?

Most people ride hybrid or mountain bikes on these trails. They both work fine, especially with conservative tires, for example semi-slick tires. A road or touring bike equipped with slightly knobby tires will also work well. However, a road bike with slick skinny racing tires isn't really suitable for this trip. More details on p. 12.

What's the trail like? Paved roads, or rough rocks, or what?

Something in between. The rail-trails on the Pittsburgh side of the mountains are mostly firmly-packed crushed limestone, with a few paved sections. The southern 15 miles of the C&O Canal Towpath, between Great Falls and Georgetown, are also crushed limestone. Most of the other 170 miles of the C&O Canal Towpath is closer to packed gravel – mostly double-track (two packed tracks with a hump between them, like a one-lane dirt road). More details on p. 12.

Can I do it?

Probably. If you can ride a bike for 30 miles on both days of a weekend, you'll do fine. We've seen families with children, youth organizations, and groups of adults of all ages. One night we shared a campsite with a 70-something gentleman who was riding from New Castle PA to Washington DC "one more time", and another night we celebrated the 80th birthday of a fellow trip member. If you aren't up to the full trip yet, plan some one-day trips this summer, a couple of weekend trips next year (itinerary ideas on p. 27), and the whole trip the year after.

Where will I sleep? Where will I eat?

There's plenty of lodging, but you should plan carefully and make reservations. Hotels, B&Bs, motels, and hostels provide indoor lodging close to the trail every 30 miles or so (list on p.38). Campgrounds are closer together, especially on the C&O Canal Towpath (list on p.36). Grocery stores and restaurants give you a choice of preparing your own food or eating someone else's cooking (locations on p.35). See our sample itineraries on p. 19 and p. 27 for ideas.

Do I need reservations?

Yes, except at some primitive trailside campsites that are designated for use by through-hikers and bikers (list on p.36). Reservations are especially important if you won't be able to drive your whole group 20 miles to an alternate motel.

How do I get to the trailhead to start the ride and then back home at the end of the trip? Where can I leave my car during the trip?

Take the train. Take a plane. Have friends drive you. Have a support car big enough to carry everything. Run a shuttle. Hire an outfitter. (Details on p. 13)

What time of year is best?

Any season except winter. Spring offers flowers but the weather can be chancy. Summer gives the longest days, but they can be hot. Fall has autumn colors and generally good weather, but days start getting short after late September. The Big Savage Tunnel is closed from late November to early April, which means you will have to shuttle on roads (see p. 16) between Frostburg and Deal during the winter.

What if it rains?

You get wet. So take a rain suit. If you plan the trip for warm weather, riding in the rain isn't horrible. It rarely rains all day for several days. If it rains for a few minutes or an hour, you can sit under shelter until it stops. We carry a small waterproof tarp to stand under. If you're camping, you can stop at the next campsite. If you have room reservations, you slog on to your motel, but you get to dry out. If it rains for days at a time, you'll probably find a motel, get dry, and consider whether to wait out the rain or cancel the rest of the trip.

Is it dangerous?

Not particularly. You should know how to fix a flat tire and recognize poison ivy. You should be able to control any children in your party. If you're camping, you should know how to pitch your tent and operate your stove safely. This is not, however, an amusement park. Everything you see is real. You can, if you choose, stand of the edges of historic structures with no safety rails. The wild animals are actually wild. There are no absolute guarantees of safety and no one else to blame for any problems. Please read the discussion of judgment and personal responsibility on p. 4.

You shouldn't have to worry about serious automobile traffic except on the Dam 4 detour and between the trail and your lodging. We recommend against biking the detours around trail gaps near Cumberland and Pittsburgh; if you ride them anyhow, you will encounter traffic – some of it heavy and fast. See discussion of detours on p. 16.

As with any physical activity, you may be at risk of overuse injuries if your activity on the trip is more strenuous than your normal routine. If you decide to skimp on advance training, plan an easy pace on the trip. If you are not already active, consult your doctor about getting started.

The Four Big Decisions: Starting to Think About the Trip

We designed this planning guide for people who want to bike the entire distance between Pittsburgh and Washington. Naturally, you don't have to ride it all at once – you can pick a shorter trip of any length you like. We offer some suggestions on shorter trips on p. 27.

Begin by making the ***Four Big Decisions*** that set the overall character of the trip.

Luxury: *What kind of overnight accommodations do we want?*

At the low end of the luxury spectrum, this is one of the finest bicycle camping trips in the east, and you can camp almost every night. At the high end of the spectrum, you can spend almost every night in a classy hotel or B&B. In between, you can use modestly priced hostels, motels or B&Bs.

Support: *How much support do we need?*

You can make this trip completely *self-contained*, carrying your clothes and, if you're camping, your cooking and sleeping gear. Alternatively, you can make it *lightly supported*, with a single vehicle to carry baggage from one night's lodging to the next. In these cases, you'll choose lodging within easy biking distance of the trail. Finally you can arrange, possibly through an outfitter (list on p. 30), for a *fully-supported* trip with someone else responsible for making all the arrangements, driving your whole group back and forth between the trail and your lodging, and perhaps even sending a guide with you on the trail.

Distance: *How far should we ride each day?*

As a practical matter, there are some stretches of 30 miles that don't have indoor lodging near the trail, so you'll have at least a few 30-mile days if you want to sleep under a roof without the complication of a fully-supported trip. Average distances of 40-45 miles per day give a nice trip of one week plus a weekend. Some people find 60 miles per day a congenial distance. There's a lot to see, and you won't ride as fast on these trails as on pavement; don't plan to ride too far each day. The distance table on p. 46 will help you plan.

Direction: *Should we ride eastbound or westbound?*

Either way works fine. The trails on the west side of Savage Mountain have smooth packed limestone surfaces and a steady gradient, downhill as you ride westbound. The towpath east of Cumberland is somewhat rougher, and it's level except for 8' rises (headed westbound) at the locks. Some folks (we're among them) prefer the terrain going westward from DC to Pittsburgh; other folks prefer to ride eastward. Another factor that may influence your decision is the problem of getting people and equipment to and from your starting and ending trailheads.

Planning Checklist

Good trips usually have someone working behind the scenes to be sure all the important arrangements are taken care of. That means, for example, knowing where you'll stay at night (or at least where the campsites are), but it does not mean knowing exactly where you'll have lunch every day or exactly what time you'll get off the trail. Here's a checklist of the major things to plan in advance.

The Four Big Decisions: Start by deciding how much *luxury* you want to pay for, how much *support* you want, what *distance* you'll ride each day, and which *direction* you'll travel. The decisions are described on p. 9.

Participants: You may start by knowing who's going, then make a plan to accommodate that group. Or you may make the plan first and then fill the trip. As the number of people increases, you need more careful planning and organization, and a group of more than 10-15 people can be unwieldy. If you plan to camp at the Hiker-Bikers along the C&O Canal, you should limit your trip size to 4 small tents or 6 people, as most of the sites are small and you might be sharing your site with several other parties.

Itinerary: Your *Big Decisions* on daily *distance* and *direction* to travel set the preliminary itinerary. After choosing distance and direction, your *Big Decision* on *luxury* determines which overnight stops can handle the number of people in your party. Unless the trip is fully supported, your choices will be limited because lodging must be within biking distance of the trail (camping on p. 36, indoor lodging on p. 38). In any case, we think biking to the overnight stop preserves the continuity of the trail experience. Make a preliminary itinerary and revise until you like the distances and locations. Use the sample itineraries on p. 19, the lodging list on p. 38, and the mileage chart on p. 46 to help. Remember to allow for the distance to lodging and meals. If you don't have enough days for the whole trip with your preferred daily distance and the available lodging, decide which part of the trip to ride and which part to save for another time.

Lodging: If you're planning to stay at hotels, motels, B&Bs, or hostels, make reservations in advance (list of places on p. 38). For lodging in smaller towns, reserve *far* in advance. Camping is more relaxed: C&O hiker-biker campsites are officially first-come-first-served, but they're shared in practice, so you won't need reservations (campgrounds on p. 36). Decide whether the trip leader will make all the reservations or distribute a hotel list for trippers to make their own.

Meals: Most towns with lodging have restaurants; the ATA web site at http://www.ATATrail.org/ has current information. Lunch is not a problem, as you'll probably pass a town with groceries or prepared food every day (list on p. 35). The grocery stores are often just convenience stores, so consider carrying an extra day's lunch. If you're camping, decide whether you'll cook as a group or individually; for group cooking decide who cooks when – and who cleans up.

Support: Your *Big Decision* on *support* determines how many vehicles and drivers you need. If you'll be riding completely *self-contained*, or if you're hiring an outfitter for full support, you don't have to worry about this. Otherwise, decide how many support vehicles you'll need and who will drive them. If you're *lightly supported*, you simply have to carry the baggage from one night's lodging to the next; you won't need to carry all the bikes and bikers. For this, one minivan is probably plenty for 6-8 people. If you chose *full support*, you need enough car, van, or trailer capacity to drive people and bikes from the trail to lodging several miles from the trail. Suggestions about these logistics are on p. 16. All your vehicles need drivers; be certain they're insured. You can find someone to drive every day, or you can share driving among the people on the trip

Transportation to and from the trail: Figure out how to get all your people, baggage, and bikes to the trailhead where you will begin your trip and how to get them home from the trailhead where you will end the trip. Advice on getting to and from the trail is on p. 13. If you leave cars at your starting trailhead, you'll need a way to get cars and people reunited. Usually this means either getting someone to drive the cars to the end or getting someone to drive the people back to the beginning. Outfitters that may be able to help move people or cars are on p. 30.

Detours around trail gaps: The trail is almost complete from McKeesport to Washington. The possible detours are discussed on p. 16

Bicycles: People usually prefer to ride their own bikes. If you need to rent bikes, try the bike shops listed on p. 34 as offering rentals. Much of the C&O Canal Towpath is too soft or too rough for a road bike with skinny tires, but you don't need all the tread of a true mountain bike tire. We recommend a hybrid or touring bike with slightly knobby hybrid tires or else a mountain bike with conservative tires, for example semi-slick tires (smooth in the center of the tread for pavement, and knobby on the edge of the tread for mud or loose sand. Be sure the riders are comfortable on the bikes, especially the seats. Be sure all the bikes are in good mechanical condition. Children are required by law to wear helmets. All bike riders should wear helmets, and laws in some areas require helmets and bells.

Sharing expenses: There's no single best way to handle expenses. Pick one in advance, make sure everyone understands it, and keep adequate records.

Trail Surface and Terrain

When you ask "what's the trail like?", you probably have two things in mind: trail surface and hills. Trail surface will make a major difference in your choice of bike. You can see photos of typical trail conditions in our trip reports for 1997 and 2001 in the Biking Trip Reports section of http://mary-shaw.org

Trail Surface

On the Great Allegheny Passage between Pittsburgh PA and Cumberland MD the trails are built on railroad grades. The finished sections are mostly smooth packed crushed limestone. A few sections are paved (asphalt).

Most of the C&O Towpath from Cumberland MD to Great Falls MD is two-track, similar to a one-lane dirt road with two packed tracks spaced about 6-8' apart and a modest hump in the middle. Some sections are better, some a bit rougher. The last 15 miles, from Great Falls MD to Washington DC, is packed crushed limestone. Detours around gaps in the trail are paved, but they have big hills.

Rain can affect trail conditions. The Great Allegheny Passage drains pretty well and isn't too bad in the rain. The towpath east from Cumberland MD to Great Falls MD gets sloppy when it rains. There will be puddles in the tracks and a few muddy sections, but it's still passable. We rode from Paw Paw WV to Hancock MD in an all-day rain on Memorial Day weekend a few years ago. We were soaked, but we didn't have trouble riding. In case of really heavy, torrential rain, certain sections of the towpath could flood, though. The National Park Service has been improving the surface, especially the soft area north of Seneca.

Hills

There are no significant hills on the finished trails. The Great Allegheny Passage sometimes has a noticeable grade, but nothing you'd call a real hill. The 22-mile climb from Cumberland to the Big Savage Mountain Tunnel is quite noticeable (about 1.5 to 1.7%). This trail is now complete from McKeesport PA to Cumberland MD, but Savage Tunnel is closed in the winter, and there are definitely hills on the winter detours around the tunnel. Instructions for this road detours are on p. 16; we do not recommend biking this.

The towpath is complete from Cumberland MD to Washington DC except for one long-standing 4-mile detour near Dam 4, south of Williamsport MD. This detour has a steep quarter-mile hill at each end – you start by riding up, ride 3 miles or so in rolling farm country, and finish by riding down. The detour route is marked, but just adequately, with small signs.

Logistics: Getting to the Trail and Home Again

Whatever you decide about support during the trip, people must get from home to the start of the trip, and they have to get back home afterward. The main options are: (a) Get friends to take you to the start and pick you up at the end. (b) Drive to the start and retrieve your cars later, either by driving back or by hiring someone to retrieve them. (c) Rent a car/van and drop it at the destination trailhead. (d) Hire someone to drive you to and from the trailheads. (e) Put bikes in boxes and take the train or plane.

Outfitter: The simplest, but perhaps the most expensive, alternative is to hire an outfitter to take you from the destination trailhead back to the beginning trailhead, or even all the way home. If you choose a fully-supported trip set up by an outfitter, you can probably arrange this as part of the trip. In other cases, you can still arrange just the shuttle with an outfitter or transportation service (p. 30). This shuttle could take you from a nearby town, airport, or train station to and from the trail, or it could take you from the end back to the beginning.

Cars: You can drive to the start of the trip. If riders use their own cars to get to the beginning trailhead, what will happen to those cars? Sometimes you can find a friend to drive riders to and from the trailheads and take the cars back home. If not, you need to find a safe place to park until you retrieve the cars after the trip.

You'll also have to get home from the destination trailhead. Sometimes friends will pick you up, too. If you parked cars at the beginning, you'll need either a ride back from the end to retrieve the cars or else someone to drive the cars to the end. Outfitters or transportation services (p. 30) may be able to transport you back or move your cars. Carpools can reduce the number of cars required. Another alternative is a one-way car rental.

If you're planning a fully-supported trip using your own support vehicles, you will probably have enough space to take everyone to the start and home from the end.

Long-term parking: You may need to leave a car parked for a few days during your trip. If you stay at a motel or B&B with ample parking the night before you start, the owner might let you leave your vehicle in their lot. In small towns, you can ask at the town hall or police station; they often allow you to park in the town lot. Washington DC, Pittsburgh PA, and other major trailhead towns have commercial parking near the trailheads, but the costs may be high. The National Park Service allows you to leave vehicles at the Great Falls, Williamsport, Hancock, and Cumberland visitor centers; register the car at the visitor center. You may also park for several days at any NPS parking lot north of Carderock (C&O 10.4) except Swains Lock; call the C&O dispatcher at 301-714-2235 so they know your plans. At McKeesport PA, the 6th St parking garage (fee) is regularly patrolled.

Train: Options for getting to and from the trail by train are limited because Amtrak only allows you take bikes as checked baggage, only on trains with baggage cars, and only to stations with baggage service. On this route, Pittsburgh PA and Washington DC are the only stations with baggage service. You must use their box and slightly dismantle the bike; be sure the train you plan to take has a baggage car. The Pittsburgh Amtrak station is a few blocks from the downtown trailhead, but bus 56C to McKeesport (p. 30) has a stop a few blocks from the Amtrack station. The Washington Amtrak station has good bike access to the trails.

To get from the Amtrak station in Pittsburgh PA to McKeesport, turn left from the Amtrak station onto Liberty Ave. In one block, turn left on Grant St. Go five blocks on Grant St to 5th Ave. From here bus 56C (p. 30) will take you to McKeesport PA. This bus runs about once an hour, and it has racks for two standard upright bikes.

To get from the Washington DC Amtrak station to MP 0 of the C&O Canal Towpath, start at the front of the Amtrak station and go southeast on Louisiana Ave half a mile to the National Mall, which runs west between Constitution and Independence Avenues. Follow the Mall west past the Washington Monument and Lincoln Memorial to the Potomac River. Do not cross the Potomac, but turn right on the wide sidewalk/bike trail. When you get to Thompson's Boat Center, turn left into the driveway. When you get to the river, turn left again between the boathouse and the river. Continue past the boathouse to Tidelock and MP 0.

If you want to bike between train stations other than Pittsburgh PA and Washington DC, one possibility is to drive to your starting point near one train station and store your bikes and baggage with someone in town, drive to your destination near another train station and park your car, then take the train back to your starting point.

Airplane: Commercial airlines serve only Pittsburgh and Washington. You can't yet ride a bike directly to or from Pittsburgh airport (the Montour Trail is working on this; check http://yockatomac.org for current information), so you'll have to use local ground transportation (page 30).

If you fly to Washington Reagan National airport, you can pick up the Mt Vernon Trail as it passes through the airport. Follow this trail north a little over 3 miles to Arlington Memorial Bridge. Cross the Potomac River on this bridge and on the other side turn left along the river. Follow the wide sidewalk/trail to Thompson Boat Center and turn left into the driveway. When you get to the river, turn left again between the boathouse and the river. Continue past the boathouse to Tidelock and MP 0.

Finding the Trailheads

Most of the time it's easy to follow the route on these trails – for example, on the C&O Towpath, keep the Potomac River on your left if you're headed to Cumberland, on your right if you're headed to Washington. However, one quirk of this route is that it's a little tricky to find the ends of the trail in McKeesport and Washington and to stay on the trail for the first mile or two (or to stay on the trail all the way to the end). Here are some hints.

McKeesport Trailhead

The McKeesport trailhead is at McKees Point Marina, on Water St near 5th Ave.

To drive there, go to McKeesport on PA148, turn west on Lysle Ave as if you were going to cross the Youghiogheny River. Just before the bridge, bear right on the ramp that descends to river level. At the bottom of the ramp, turn left on Water St. Alternatively, take the 56C bus from downtown (it has racks for two upright bikes).

To get onto the Great Allegheny Passage from McKees Point Marina, follow Water St to 9th Ave. At the circle, follow the limestone trail until it ends at a road, follow that road, get back onto the trail when it resumes, and stay on the limestone as it twists through town. Bear left at the fork to the 15th St bridge, cross the bridge, take the first left and the next right onto River Rd. At the end of the road, follow the trail on the right side of the street.

To find McKees Point Marina from the trail, follow the trail around the pipe plant, follow River Rd to the 15th St Bridge, cross the bridge on the far sidewalk, follow the limestone trail to the Marina, which is at the mouth of the river.

Washington Trailhead

The Washington trailhead is on the south (downstream) side of Thompson's Boat House at the mouth of Rock Creek.

To drive there, find your way to Thompson Boat Center (directions at http://www.thompsonboatcenter.com/direct.htm). From the parking lot, follow the road to the boathouse, then go around the boathouse to the mouth of Rock Creek.

To get onto the C&O Canal Towpath from Thompson Boat Center, go around the boathouse to the parking lot. Turn left on the sidewalk next to the road. Follow the sidewalk across two roads and a bridge across Rock Creek. Immediately after crossing the creek, turn left down a short hill on the brick towpath.

To find Thompson Boat Center from the trail, follow the trail along the canal until the brick towpath climbs to a sidewalk. Turn right, follow the sidewalk to Thompson Boat Center, and go around the boathouse to the mouth of Rock Creek.

Logistics: Local Transportation During the Trip

Trail gaps

There are three detours between Pittsburgh and Washington: Nine miles remain unfinished between Pittsburgh and McKeesport. From November to April, Big Savage Tunnel is closed, requiring a detour. A long-standing detour around Dam 4 between C&O mileposts 85 and 88 is bicycleable. Driving directions for these detours are at http://yockatomac.org/linkup/detour.htm. We do not recommend biking on the two Great Allegheny Passage detours.

Self-contained trips

On a self-contained trip, bikers carry all their own gear and ride to the campsite or lodging. No vehicle accompanies the trip. That means that your only transportation problem during the trip is getting people and gear around the detours. If you start or end in McKeesport and go when Big Savage Tunnel is open, you should be ok.

Lightly-supported trips

On a lightly-supported trip, you need a vehicle to carry baggage from one night's lodging to the next. This vehicle can probably carry some (but not all) people and bikes to and from the trailheads. You need a driver for this vehicle. You may be fortunate enough to have a volunteer – perhaps a friend or family member who doesn't want to bike all day. People on the trip can drop out for half a day at a time to drive. Or you can hire a driver. For detours around trail gaps, you can make multiple trips, or pre-position one of your own cars nearby, or hire a local shuttle service, or let some bikers ride the roads (carefully!). If you're camping, note that the many hiker-biker campgrounds are intended for groups of six or fewer through-bikers, and they're deliberately located far away from car access. There are some campgrounds with car access, but they're farther apart (see p. 36).

Fully-supported trips

On a fully-supported trip, you need enough vehicles and drivers to carry all the people, baggage, and bikes back and forth between the trail and your lodging (B&B, motel or commercial campground). This could be a large van with trailer or several cars. You'll also be able to drive everyone to and from the trailheads and on the detours around trail gaps. The advantage is that you can avoid riding on roads, and you get many more options for lodging and dining. The disadvantage is that you may spend a lot of time organizing, waiting for people, loading, unloading, and driving. This extra complexity seems to us to detract from the trail experience, especially the sense of riding a continuous trail.

Preparation

Physical conditioning

You certainly don't have to be a serious athlete, but you will be riding moderate distances on several successive days. So it's a good idea to do some riding in advance. In particular, it's a good idea to ride two or three days in a row a few times. Some of your preparation rides should be as long as the daily distances you plan for the trip. However, we have ridden this trip with a few people who did fine with almost no advance preparation.

Itinerary, reservations, and support

If you're planning an unsupported camping trip, planning is minimal – just load up the bikes, take a list of campgrounds, and start out. However, if you want to sleep indoors, you should make reservations at B&Bs or motels that suit your *Big Decision* about *luxury* and provide reasonable daily riding distances (list on p. 38). You also need to think about logistics for the trip and plans for transporting people between home and the beginning and end of the trip; see page 13.

Bicycles and bicycle preparation

Our groups have used a variety of bikes, including suspended mountain bikes, hybrids, tandems, recumbents, and old beater road bikes. Friends with hybrids have done fine on fully loaded camping trips. Most folks with mountain bikes prefer conservative tires with a little tread in the center and lugs on the edges to handle mud. If you do your own maintenance, check the bike over before leaving. If you don't do your own, take the bike to your friendly local bike shop for a safety check and tune-up – then ride it on a short trip to be sure everything's ok. Be sure you are comfortable on the bike, especially the seat. Check your helmet, too – you'll be wearing it for a week.

Baggage and camping equipment preparation

If you're carrying baggage on your bikes, be sure you can carry it all safely and under control. Get racks and decent panniers. If you have camping gear, you'll probably find that the bike handles better if you split the load between front and back panniers. You might also consider a one-wheeled cargo trailer. We don't think the C&O Canal towpath is suitable for 2-wheeled trailers, but other people have said they're fine.

Be sure you know how to operate all your camping equipment. We've been entertained for untold hours by watching people take new tents and camp stoves out of their factory packages after dark and try to set them up in campsites far from home. Don't join the entertainers.

What to Take

Many bicycle guides offer suggestions about what to pack for a bike tour. Here's our version; if you like one of the others, that's fine too.

Clothes and personal items in overnight baggage

Clothes to ride in	Toilet kit	Warm shirt or windbreaker
Clothes for hotel or camp	Wallet, ID, money	Long-sleeved shirt, long pants
Extra shoes	Notebook, pen for journal	Hat with brim

Choose clothes based on the weather you expect – but take an additional warm layer. One night is likely to be 10-15 degrees colder than you expect.

Personal items for daily use (carry with you or wear)

Helmet	Camera, film or cards	First aid kit
Gloves	Guidebook	Insect repellent
Water bottles/hydration pack	Jacket or sweater	Sunscreen
Rain gear	Swim suit, wading shoes	Sunglasses
Waterproof tarp (5'x7')	Plastic bags	Toilet paper
Snack or energy bar	Pocket knife	Cell phone (emergency use)

Carry at least a quart more water than you think you need.

Bike equipment

Bike	Patch kit, tire levers	Handlebar pack
Bike lock	Spare tube	Rack
Headlight, taillight	Pump	Rack pack or panniers
Bell or whistle	Tools (know how to use 'em)	Rain cover for panniers
Fenders	Spokes (to fit your wheels)	Bungee cords

We don't recommend carrying more than a few pounds in a backpack. Your load will be much more stable in panniers on a rack firmly attached to the bike. If you're camping or traveling without vehicle support for more than a few days, split the load between front and back panniers for better handling. Many people prefer a trailer; a one-wheeled trailer such as the BOB works well on the C&O.

Even if you don't plan to ride after dark, you'll want the headlight or a flashlight in the Paw Paw tunnel (C&O MP 155).

Camping equipment

Tent	Stove, matches	Towel
Sleeping bag	Cook kit, utensils	Plastic ziplock bags
Sheet or sleeping bag liner	Food (carry an extra meal)	Biodegradable soap
Air mattress or sleeping pad	Extra water	

Oh, yes – did we mention extra water?

Sample Itineraries

Here are six sample itineraries for the full trip, illustrating both directions and various lodging options: B&Bs, motels, camping, and hostels (low-cost housing for trippers with bunkrooms and shared kitchen facilities and common area). One shows how to make the full trip in four long weekends. More details on places to stay appear here on pp. 36 and 38 and on the Allegheny Trail Alliance web site at http://www.ATATrail.org/ Use these itineraries as starting points for your own planning. See p. 5 for a list of trail abbreviations.

The mileages are distance along the trail, not including distance to lodging.

Lightly-supported 11-day B&B/motel trip from Leesburg VA to Washington DC to Pittsburgh PA

This is a slight update of the itinerary of Yockatomac trek '99, the June 1999 inaugural trip of the Allegheny Trail Alliance. We used a van to carry baggage each day; a volunteer drove the van for the whole trip. The van wasn't large enough to carry all the riders and bikes, so we selected lodging within easy biking distance of the trail. Several riders wanted to see the Washington and Old Dominion Trail in Virginia, so we started a day early to add the W&OD. You could certainly start in Washington DC instead. This revision reflects the new trail sections since 1999.

Date	*Segment*	*Lodging*	*Distance*
Fri	Pittsburgh to Leesburg by car, W&OD Leesburg to Purcellville and return for those who arrived early	Days Inn, Leesburg VA	24 miles optional
Sat	Leesburg to Washington DC via W&OD, 4MiRn & AndBW; MtVer; and C&O	Georgetown Inn, Washington DC	44 miles
Sun	Washington DC to Leesburg via CapCr, C&O, and Whites Ferry. Be extremely careful in traffic going to Leesburg	Days Inn, Leesburg VA	36 miles
Mon	Leesburg to Shepherdstown via C&O. Be careful in traffic returning from Leesburg	Thomas Shepherd Inn, Shepherdstown WV	37 miles
Tue	Shepherdstown to Hancock via C&O and WMRT	Super 8, Hancock MD	51 miles
Wed	Hancock to Paw Paw via C&O	Heritage Trail B&B. Paw Paw WV	32 miles
Thu	Paw Paw to Cumberland via C&O	Inn at Walnut Bottom, Cumberland MD	28 miles
Fri	Cumberland to Meyersdale via Western Md Scenic RR and GAP	Burgess House, Meyersdale PA	32 miles
Sat	Meyersdale to Ohiopyle via GAP	Yough Plaza Motel, Ohiopyle PA	42 miles
Sun	Ohiopyle to Smithton via GAP	Fairway Inn	36 miles
Mon	Smithton to McKeesport via GAP, car shuttle to Hazelwood, GAP to Pittsburgh	return home	25 miles

Fully-supported 7-day trip from Pittsburgh PA to Washington DC

Let someone else do the driving. Take the train to Pittsburgh PA and home from Washington DC. The train from Philadelphia arrives early afternoon; adjust the first day's sightseeing for other trains. This includes the classic 3-day C&O trip.

Date	*Segment*	*Lodging*	*Distance*
Sun	Amtrak to Pittsburgh, arriving early afternoon. Tour Pittsburgh. Eliza Furnace Trail to Oakland for overnight	Motel in Oakland	5-15 mi
Mon	Get a ride to McKeesport. Bike GAP to Connellsville	Melody Motor Lodge	44 miles
Tue	Connellsville to Rockwood via GAP	Rockwood Trail House B&B	47 miles
Wed	Rockwood to Frostburg (29 miles), GAP or scenic RR to Cumberland (15 Miles)	Inn at Walnut Bottom B&B	28 or 44 miles
Thu	Cumberland to Hancock via C&O	Super 8	60 miles
Fri	Hancock to Harpers Ferry via C&O	Hilltop House or B&B	63 mi
Sat	Harpers Ferry to Georgetown via C&O		61 miles

Self-contained 8-day camping trip from DC to Pittsburgh

This is a variant of a trip that several of us made in the spring of 2006. We parked in McKeesport and hired an outfitter to drive us to Washington DC. The long day from Cumberland to Confluence reflects the lack of campsites on the stretch.

Date	*Segment*	*Lodging*	*Distance*
Sat	Stage shuttle via Cumberland to DC, ride to Horsepen Branch on C&O	Horsepen Branch Hiker-Biker C&O 26.0	26 miles
Sun	Horsepen Branch to Antietam via C&O	Antietam Walk-in C&O 69.4	43 miles
Mon	Antietam to North Mountain via C&O	North Mtn Hiker-Biker C&O 110.0	41 miles
Tue	North Mountain to Stickpile Hill via C&O	Stickpile Hill Hiker-Biker C&O 149.4	39 miles
Wed	Stickpile Hill to Cumberland via C&O	Cumberland YMCA C&0 184.5, GAP 0	35 miles
Thu	Cumberland MD to Frostburg Train (16 miles) Frostburg to Confluence via GAP (47 mi) – long day!	Yough Dam Outflow Camping GAP 62	47 miles
Fri	Confluence to Round Bottom via GAP	Round Bottom primitive camp, GAP 99	37 miles
Sat	Round Bottom to McKeesport via GAP	At home GAP 132	33 miles

Self-contained 5- or 10-day motel/hostel trip from Pittsburgh to DC

For a more leisurely trip, this 30-mile/day itinerary uses inexpensive lodging where it can and doesn't require any support – just pack your clothes on your bike and go. For a fast trip (60 miles/day), use every other stop on this itinerary. This is a natural extension of the popular 3-day, 60-mile/day itinerary for the C&O Canal. For economy, stay at hostels at Meyersdale and Sandy Hook and the bikers bunkhouse in Hancock. To shorten the first day, start at Boston.

Date	*Segment*	*Lodging*	*30mpd*	*60mpd*
Sat	McKeesport to Connellsville via GAP	Connellsville PA	44 mi	72 mi
Sun	Connellsville to Confluence via GAP	Confluence PA	28 mi	
Mon	Confluence to Meyersdale (hostel) via GAP	Meyersdale PA	28 mi	60 mi
Tue	Meyersdale to Cumberland via GAP	Cumberland MD	32 mi	
Wed	Cumberland to Paw Paw via C&O	Paw Paw WV	28 mi	60 mi
Thu	Paw Paw to Hancock (bike shop bunkhouse) via C&O	Hancock MD	32 mi	
Fri	Hancock to Williamsport via C&O	Williamsport MD	24 mi	63 mi
Sat	Williamsport to Harpers Fy/Sandy Hook (hostel) via C&O	Sandy Hook MD	39 mi	
Sun	Sandy Hook to Leesburg via C&O	Leesburg VA	25 mi	61 mi
Mon	Leesburg to Washington DC via C&O	Washington DC	36 mi	

Lightly-supported 8-day camping trip from DC to Pittsburgh

This trip is similar to the camping trip above, except we used a support van to transport the camping gear, so we used car-accessible camping wherever it's available (everywhere except Leesburg).

Date	*Segment*	*Lodging*	*Distance*
Sun	Washington DC to Leesburg via CapCr, C&O, and Whites Ferry Be extremely careful in traffic to Leesburg	Days Inn, Leesburg VA (C&O 35.5 + 5 miles)	42 miles
Mon	Leesburg VA to Shepherdstown WV via C&O Be careful in traffic leaving Leesburg	Antietam Walk-in camp, C&O 69.4 + 5 miles)	39 miles
Tue	Shepherdstown WV to Hancock MD via C&O and WMRT	Ft Frederick SP camp, C&O 112.4	44 miles
Wed	Hancock MD to Paw Paw WV via C&O	Paw Paw Walk-in camp, C&O 156.2	45 miles
Thu	Paw Paw WV to Cumberland MD via C&O	Cumberland YMCA C&O 185, GAP 0	30 miles
Fri	Cumberland MD to Frostburg Train (16 miles) Frostburg to Confluence via GAP (47 mi)	Yough Dam Outflow Camping GAP 62	47 miles
Sat	Confluence PA to Cedar Creek Park PA via GAP	Cedar Creek camp GAP 110	48 miles
Sun	Cedar Creek Park PA to McKeesport PA via GAP	return home GAP 132	22 miles

The whole trail, in easy pieces

Four long weekends with 30-mile days

If you can't arrange to take a week or so for the trip, you can still see the whole trail in a series of long weekends. Here's one way to do it, with most days in the 25-35 mile range. You can pick up the finished trail in Pittsburgh as a one-day trip.

Trip 1: Downhill on the Great Allegheny Passage: Rockwood PA to McKeesport PA. Use two or more cars. Park one at McKeesport PA the night before you leave or on the first morning. Drive to Rockwood PA and park the others at the trailhead. Spend the first night at Ohiopyle PA and the second at Smithton PA. This gives you daily mileages of 30, 36, and 25 miles, plus a few miles back and forth to your lodging. When you get to McKeesport, use the car you left there to take the drivers of the other cars back to Rockwood.

Trip 2: Through the Mountain: Rockwood, PA to Cumberland MD. Meet at the trailhead in Rockwood MD. Put two changes of clothes on the bike. Spend the first night in Frostburg. In the morning, ride the 15 miles (all down hill) to Cumberland to catch the train at 11:00 to return to Frostburg with your bike. In the afternoon, tour the Thrasher Carriage Museum. Spend the night in Frostburg and return to your car the next day. This gives you daily mileages of 28, 16, and 28 plus a few miles back and forth to your lodging. You will need to reserve space on the train for your bike. Note: The train does not run every day.

Trip 3: Upper C&O Towpath: Cumberland MD to Williamsport MD. Use two or more cars. Meet at the trailhead in Cumberland MD. Drive all the cars to the NPS visitor center in Williamsport, park all but one there, and return to Cumberland in the other. Stay in Paw Paw WV the first night and Hancock MD the second night, giving daily mileages of 28, 32, and 24 miles, plus a few miles back and forth to your lodging. When you get to Williamsport, either retrieve the car you left in Cumberland or cram all your gear into the car(s) you left at Williamsport and take everyone to Cumberland.

Trip 4: Lower C&O Towpath: Williamsport MD to Washington DC. Use two or more cars. It's hard to find good, cheap parking in Washington DC, so position one car somewhere in the Georgetown area. Meet at the NPS visitor center in Williamsport and leave the rest of the cars there. Spend the first night in Harpers Ferry WV and the second near Whites Ferry MD, perhaps in Leesburg VA, giving daily mileages of 39, 25, and 36 miles, plus a few miles back and forth to your lodging. When you get to Georgetown, use the car you left there to take the drivers of the other cars back to Williamsport.

Excursions

You may want to vary your trip by including a detour to an interesting site near the trail, or perhaps a short day and optional excursion, or a rest day with something to do. We can't provide a complete list, of course. These are among our favorites, and they're bike-accessible from the trail without additional transportation.

Washington DC (C&O 0): "The Mall" The major historical and monument area, between the Lincoln Memorial and the Capital, is bike-friendly. The Washington and Jefferson Memorials are also nearby, as is one of our favorites, the statue of Albert Einstein on the grounds of the National Academy of Science at 22nd and Constitution. Consider staying an extra day or two in Washington for biking as well as sightseeing. You can take a day trip to Mt Vernon down the Mt Vernon Trail on the Virginia side of the Potomac River or ride a loop up the Capital Crescent and back down Rock Creek (the park road is mostly closed to traffic on Sundays).

White's Ferry (C&O 35): Ride the only remaining cable ferry on the Potomac.

Rileys Lockhouse Tour (C&O 22.8): On weekend afternoons, Girl Scouts offer tours of the lockhouse.

Point of Rocks MD (C&O 48.2): Visit the historic Point of Rocks RR station.

Harpers Ferry WV (C&O 60.7): Either lock your bike at the foot of the stairs or carry it up, then cross the pedestrian bridge. You come out in Harpers Ferry National Historical Park, where you can visit buildings and sites associated with the Civil War. Get more information at http://www.nps.gov/hafe/

Sharpsburg MD (C&O 69.3): Leave the Towpath at Antietam Village and ride up the hill to Antietam Battlefield, site of one of the bloodiest battles of the Civil War. Get more information at http://www.nps.gov/anti/

Fort Frederick (C&O 112.4): America's premier stone French & Indian War fort.

Cumberland MD (C&O 184.5): Plan some time to visit the Canal Place restoration and the Western Maryland Scenic RR. Combine the scenic railroad with your trip by riding the train one way between Cumberland and Frostburg. You may take your bike on the train, but reserve space for your bike in advance.

Frostburg MD (GAP 15): Tour the Thrasher Carriage Museum right next door to the railroad station.

Ohiopyle PA (GAP 72): Visit the falls, hike the trails or go whitewater rafting. Two Frank Lloyd Wright houses are nearby, but you'll need a ride to get there.

Pittsburgh PA (GAP 149): Before leaving town, ride the riverfront trails.

Overview Map of Trail

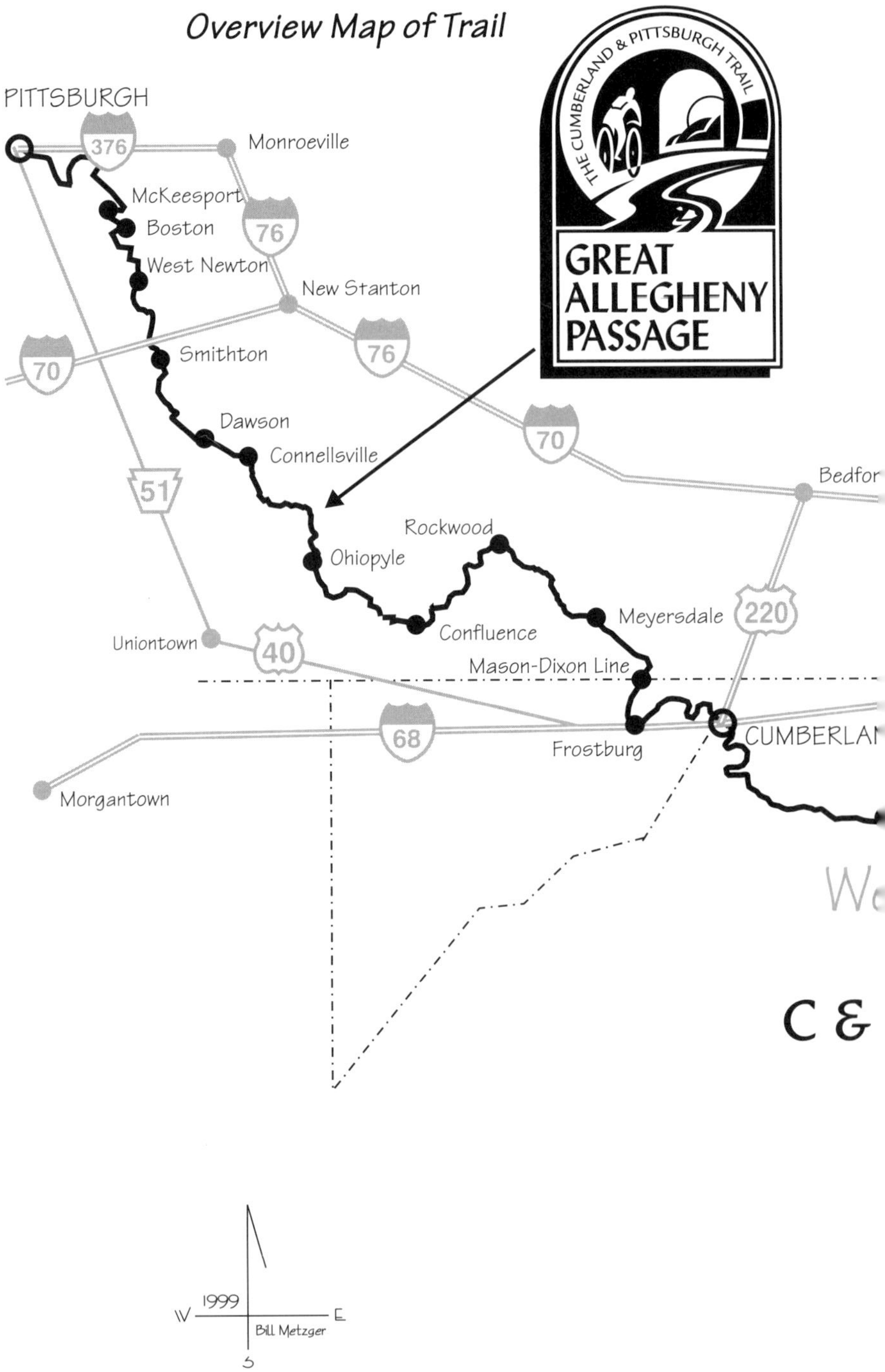

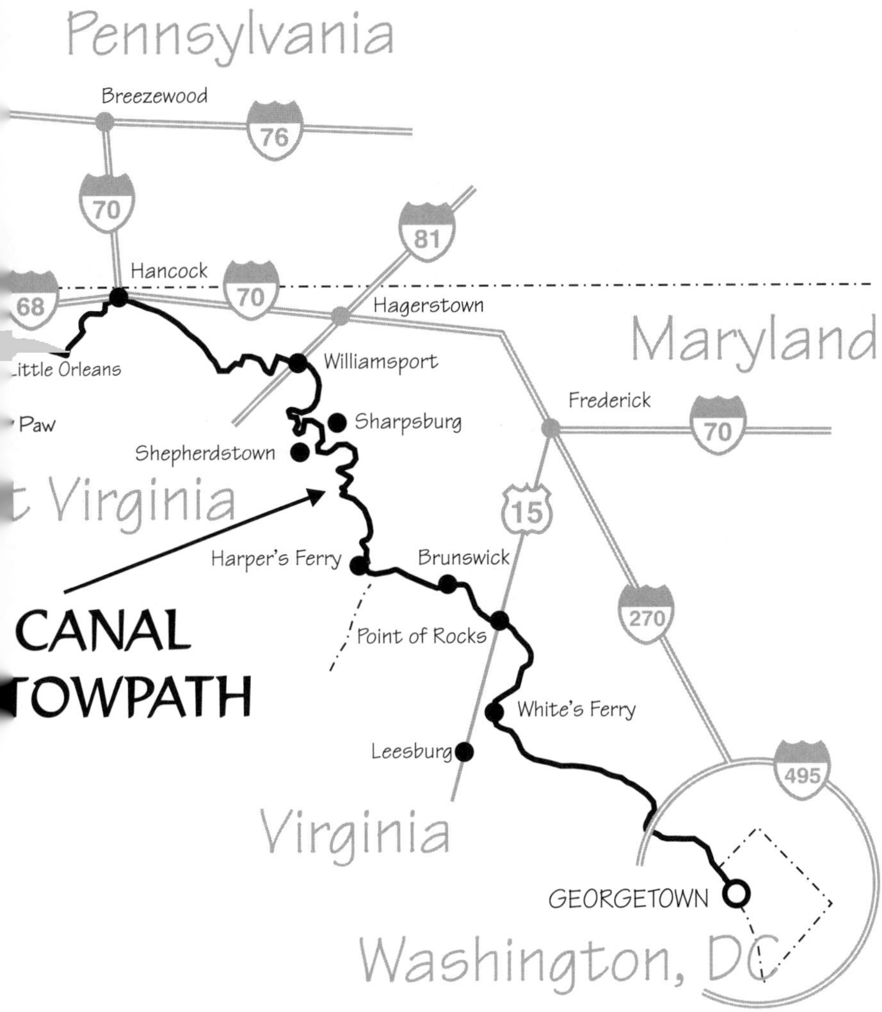
Pennsylvania
Breezewood
76
70
81
68
Hancock
70
Hagerstown
Maryland
Little Orleans
Williamsport
Frederick
70
Paw
Sharpsburg
Shepherdstown
Virginia
15
Harper's Ferry
Brunswick
CANAL
TOWPATH
Point of Rocks
270
White's Ferry
Leesburg
495
Virginia
GEORGETOWN
Washington, DC

Resources

On-Line Information

The *Allegheny Trail Alliance* web site, http://www.ATATrail.org/ has trail maps, lists of amenities and services along the trail.

The *Yockatomac Trek* web site http://yockatomac.org has itineraries, trip reports and planning advice.

The *Linking Up* web site http://yockatomac.org/linkup has the on-line version of this information. It gets updated before the book is updated.

Books and Maps

FreeWheeling Easy in Western Pennsylvania by Mary Shaw and Roy Weil. A guide to over 46 traffic-free trails in Western Pennsylvania. Provides descriptions, maps, directions to trailheads, and information on local amenities. Currently (May 2007) out of print. New edition available Fall 2007 from Shaw-Weil Associates, 414 S Craig St, Pittsburgh, PA 15213. $21+tax+s/h. Also available from amazon.com.

The Great Allegheny Passage Companion: A Guide to History & Heritage along the Trail from McKeesport to Meyersdale by Bill Metzger. Detailed annotations for the trail, plus essays on local and railroad history. Available from The Local History Company $19.95+tax+s/h (866-362-0789) and amazon.com.

Great Little Walks in the Pittsburgh Area by Yvonne Merrill with Mary Shaw. Gives detailed information and maps on casual walks and short bike rides on the traffic-free Great Allegheny Passage and connecting trails. Available from Alleghany Trail Alliance, $7.95+tax+s/h (888-ATA-BIKE) and amazon.com

Trail Book 2007. Provides information on businesses and services available along the trail. Available from Allegheny Trail Alliance, $5+tax+s/h (888-ATA-BIKE)

Towpath Guide to the C&O Canal by Thomas F. Hahn, available from C&O Canal visitor centers for $15+tax+s/h. Detailed description of the features along C&O Canal Towpath. Available from C&O Towpath Visitor centers.

The C&O Canal Companion by Mike High, Johns Hopkins University Press, $15.95+tax+s/h. More contemporary, but less detailed, than Hahn. Available from amazon.com.

Washington DC Regional Bike Map, by ADC (The Map People), 6440 General Green Way, Alexandria VA 22312. The 6th edition (2004) was $8.95. Map of DC area showing bike trails and on-road bike routes.

Shorter Trips

While the entire trip is a wonderful experience, it's perfectly all right to ride a shorter portion. You might do this because you have only a weekend or a long weekend rather than a week, because you aren't sure about embarking on a long bike trip, or simply because that's all you want to do. You can plan your own trips using the trail mileage table (p. 46) and list of lodging (p. 38) or camping (p. 36). Current information on services near the trail is at http://www.ATATrail.org/. As examples to get you started, here are a few short trips that you may enjoy.

A sweet, scenic B&B getaway: Connellsville to Confluence and back

(2 to 4 days, B&B, 30 miles per day)

Park at the Connellsville trailhead (GAP 89) and load lunch and your change of clothes on your bikes. Ride southward. Eat lunch at the Yough River overlook (GAP 79). Have ice cream at Ohiopyle (GAP 72). Continue to Confluence (GAP 62), taking the first bridge across the Youghiogheny River. Turn left after crossing the river and follow the road 4 blocks to River's Edge B&B. Have dinner at River's Edge and stay there or in one of the other nearby B&Bs overnight. Return the next day by retracing your steps.

To make this a 3-day weekend, reserve your room in Confluence for 2 nights and ride out toward Rockwood (GAP 43) and back to Confluence on the second day; you can make this day as long or as short as you wish. Return to Connellsville on the third day.

To make this a 4-day weekend, reserve your room in Confluence for the first and third nights and reserve a room in Meyersdale (GAP 32) for the second night.

Overnight over the mountain: Rockwood to Frostburg and back

(2 days, B&B, 31 miles per day)

Park at the Rockwood trailhead (GAP 43) and load lunch and your change of clothes on your bikes. Ride southward. Eat lunch at the South end of the Savage Tunnel overlooking the Cumberland Narrows (GAP 22). Continue to Frostburg, taking the switch backs up to the railroad station and on into town. Have dinner at Tombstone Cafe and stay overnight at Trail Inn or Failinger's Hotel Gunter. Return the next day by retracing your steps. This trip can be shortened by starting at Garrett (GAP 36) or Meyersdale (GAP 32) or lengthened by starting at Markleton (GAP 50) or Harnedsville (GAP 59) or by staying in Cumberland (GAP 0).

Introduction to bicycle camping: Boston to Round Bottom and back

(2 days, camping, 29 miles per day)

Park at the Boston trailhead (GAP 128) and load your camping gear on your bikes. Ride southward, with the river on your left. Pack a picnic lunch or eat in West Newton (GAP 114). Camp at Round Bottom Campground beside the trail (GAP 100). Return to Boston the next day.

A long weekend on the Towpath: Cumberland to Hancock

(3 days, camping or B&B/motel, 20-30 miles per day)

Take enough people to justify two cars. Meet in Cumberland (C&O 184.5) and unload your bikes and gear. Drive both cars to Hancock, 40 miles on I68. Leave one car at the C&O visitor center at the east end of town and bring both drivers back in the other car.

For indoor lodging, spend the first night in Paw Paw and the second night at the Super 8 in Hancock. The third day, ride down the Western MD Rail-Trail to Ernstville Rd, cross over to the towpath, and return to Hancock (and your car) on the towpath.

For a camping trip, set out and camp wherever you are when it's time to stop, probably at the Town Creek (C&O 162.1) or Purslane Run (C&O 157.4) hiker-biker. The second day, camp wherever you are when it's time to stop – probably Indigo Neck (C&O 139.2), Cacapon Jct (C&O 133.6), or White Rock (C&O 126.4) hiker-biker. The third day, leave your camping gear in the car as you go by, continue on the Western Maryland Rail Trail, and return on the towpath to make a full day.

A two- or three-day loop near the Nation's Capital: Leesburg to Washington and return

(2 or 3 days, B&B/hotel, 40-45 miles per day)

Friday evening, drive to Leesburg VA (4-5 hours drive from Pittsburgh but less than an hour from DC) and check into your B&B (for example, Norris House) or motel (for example, Days Inn). Saturday morning pack a change of clothes on your bike, ride south a few blocks to the Washington & Old Dominion Trail and turn left (east). Follow the W&OD about 35 miles to its end in Shirlington, then pick your way 3-4 blocks around city streets to the bike/ped bridge over the highway. On the other side of the bridge follow city streets to pick up Four-Mile Run Trail to the Potomac River and turn left on Mt Vernon Trail. The Washington DC Regional Bike Map will be very helpful for finding these trail connections.

Take the Mt Vernon Trail to the Arlington Memorial Bridge and cross the Potomac River. If you're staying at a hotel in Georgetown (for example, The Latham or

Georgetown Inn), follow the waterfront left (upstream) past Thompson Boat Center and turn left on the C&O Canal Towpath in Georgetown, near your hotel. If you're staying at the Washington Hostel, after crossing the Arlington Memorial Bridge go past the Lincoln Memorial and down The Mall to 12th St, then go up 12th St 7 blocks to K St, then right a block to the Hostel.

Sunday morning return to the C&O Canal Towpath (via K and M Sts if you stay at the Hostel) and head out the towpath. Go out the towpath to Whites Ferry (C&O 35.5) and take the ferry across the Potomac River. Climb the hill and turn left on US15 (busy traffic, alas). Follow US15, then Business US15 into Leesburg to retrieve your car.

For a three-day trip, spend Sunday visiting the memorials in Washington or ride down the Mt Vernon Trail 20 miles to (where else?) Mt Vernon and back. Then return to Leesburg on Monday.

Outfitters and Shuttle Services

Some people can arrange their own transportation to and from the trailheads or around trail gaps. Others may prefer to pay someone to drive their groups. When the cost is shared among the members of the group, it may be quite reasonable. Similarly, some people will prefer to make their own hotel reservations, and others may prefer to have that done by someone more experienced. Some of these outfitters will arrange fully-outfitted trips as well as shuttles. We are not personally familiar with most of these services. We present this information for your convenience; it is not a review or recommendation.

A&A Transportations, Hagerstown MD
    301-416-7872
Shuttle for all points between Washington DC and Pittsburgh PA for up to 10 people with bikes. Need at least one week notice.

Allegany Expeditions, I68 Exit 45 east of Cumberland
    800-819-5170
    info@alleganyexpeditions.com
    http://www.alleganyexpeditions.com
Shuttles for all points between Washington DC and Meyersdale PA by prior arrangement.

Allegany Limousine, Cumberland MD
    301-777-3200
Shuttles for all points between Washington DC and Pittsburgh PA. Need 14 days notice.

Bill's Taxis (Yellow Cab drivers), Pittsburgh PA
    412-855-4484
Local taxi service in Pittsburgh area, including airport, train station, McKeesport-Boston. Call a day ahead to make arrangements to carry bikes

C&O Bicycles, Hancock MD
    301-678-6665
    http://www.candobycycle.com
Shuttle from Hancock to Washington D.C for up to 5 people and bikes. Need at least 48 hours notice.

Ducky's, Hagerstown MD
    301-331-1488
Need at least two hours notice. Can transport bikes.

Freedom Trail Riders, Glen Burnie MD, Cumberland MD
301-707-6097 (PA, western MD), 443-867-0835 (eastern MD. DC)
freedomtrailriders@yahoo.com
http://www.freedomtrailriders.com

Shuttles and other support along the C&O Canal, the Great Allegheny Passage, and other regional trail systems. Must arrange in advance.

Get Out & Go Tours, LLC, Ashburn, VA
703-728-8665
info@getoutandgo.biz
http://www.getoutandgo.biz

Fully-supported 5-day bike trips between DC and Pittsburgh. Fully-supported 3-day C&O Canal Tours between DC and Cumberland.

Kewl Tourism and Shuttles, Hagerstown, MD
301-898-8628

Shuttles for up to 50 people with bikes. Need 3 to 7 days notice.

Laurel Highlands River Tours, Ohiopyle PA
800-OHIOPYLE or 800-4-RAFTEN
4raftin@laurelhighlands.com
http://www.laurelhighlands.com

Scheduled shuttle for selected points on Great Allegheny Passage.

Mountainside Bike Tours, Cumberland, MD
800-459-0510, 240-727-7039
mountainsidebikes@gmail.com
http://www.mountainsidebiketours.net

Bike tour packages along the C&O Canal and the Great Allegheny Passage

Port Authority of Allegheny County, Pittsburgh PA
412-442-2000
http://www.portauthority.org/

Busses on several routes have bike racks for two standard upright bikes. Route 56C (http://www.portauthority.org/PAAC/apps/pdfs/56C.pdf) has bike racks and runs approximately hourly between downtown Pittsburgh and McKeesport.

Queen City Taxi, Cumberland MD
301-722-2800

Shuttles between Meyersdale and Cumberland, by prior arrangement.

River & Trail Outfitters, Knoxville MD

301-695-5177

river@rivertrail.com

http://www.rivertrail.com

Main business is river trips, they have done biking shuttles for groups in the Harpers Ferry WV area. Must make arrangements in advance

River Riders, Harpers Ferry,

800-326-7238 or 304-535-2663

trips@riverriders.com

http://www.riverriders.com

Can shuttle bikes as well, four person minimum.

Time Advantage, Hagerstown MD

301-393-5714

http://www.timeadvantage.net

Can transport up to 4 people with bikes. Need at least 1 day notice.

Western Maryland Adventures Shuttle Service, Flintstone MD

301-784-8403

info@wmdadventures.com

http://www.wmdadventures.com

Custom shuttle service by prior arrangement.

Western Maryland Scenic RR, Cumberland MD

301-759-4400, 800-TRAIN-50

wmsrinfo@wmsr.com

http://www.wmsr.com

Scenic railroad from Cumberland MD to Frostburg MD, accepts bikes on the train.

West Newton Bicycle Shop, West Newton PA

724-872-2185

Shuttle service from West Newton to anywhere, Memorial Day to Labor Day.

WestMar Tours and Travel, Cumberland MD

800-336-7963

westmartours@mindsping.com

http://www.wstmr.com

Mostly bus tours, but will help bicyclists with shuttles, limit 2 people with bikes. Must make prior arrangements.

Wilderness Voyageurs, Ohiopyle PA
724-329-8336, 800-272-4141
http://www.wilderness-voyageurs.com

Fully-supported 6-day bike trips from DC to Pittsburgh. Shuttles for up to 14 people with bikes for points between McKeesport PA and Cumberland MD. Must make arrangements in advance

Youghiogheny Canoe Outfitters, West Newton PA
724-872-7585
http://www.youghcanoe.com

Can transport up to 15 people, bikes, canoes. Need one week advance notice.

Yough River Transport, Dunbar PA
724-277-0550
info@youghrivertransport.com
http://youghrivertransport.com

Shuttles along the Great Allegheny Passage and the C&O Canal. For up to 16 people, bicycles, and equipment. Need one week advance notice.

Bike Shops

In case of mechanical trouble, it's nice to know about the bike shops near the trail. Not all shops that rent bikes will rent for multi-day trips.

Trail, MP	Business	Address	City	Phone	Bike Rent
C&O 0	Thompson's Boat Cntr	Rk Ck Pkwy & Va NW	DC	202-333-9543	Yes
C&O 0	Bike the Sites	Penn. & Constitution	DC	202-966-8662	Yes
C&O 1	Big Wheel Bikes	1034 33rd St NW	DC	202-337-0254	Yes
C&O 1	Revolution Cycles	3411 M St NW	DC	202-965-3601	No
C&O 3	Fletcher's Boat Center	4940 Canal Rd	DC	202-244-0461	Yes
C&O 55	Brunswick Hardware	302 W Potomac St	Brunswick	301-834-9207	No
C&O 55	C&O Canal Biking	24 W Potomac St	Brunswick	301-834-5180	Yes
C&O 60	River & Trail Outfitters	604 Valley Rd	Knoxville	301-695-5177	Yes
C&O 61	Outfitter at Harpers Fy	189 High St	Harpers Ferry	888-535-2087	Yes
C&O 61	River Riders	408 Allstadts Hill Rd.	Harpers Ferry	800-326-7238	Yes
C&O 80	Reels & Wheels	17328 Taylors Lndg Rd	Sharpsburg	301-432-7281	No
C&O 100	River City Cycles	22 N Conococheague	Williamsport	301-223-6733	
C&O 124	C&O Bicycle	9 S Pennsylvania Av	Hancock	301-678-6665	Yes
C&O 185	Cycles & Things	165 N Centre St	Cumberland	301-722-5496	No
C&O 185	Mountainside Bike Trs	108 Decatur St	Cumberland	800-459-0510	Yes
GAP 15	Adventure Sport (24/7)	115 E Main St	Frostburg	301-689-0345	Yes
GAP 43	Rockwood Trail House	131 Rockdale Rd	Rockwood	814-916-2453	Yes
GAP 62	Allegheny Recumbents	P.O. Box 160	Confluence	888-395-BIKE	Yes
GAP 62	Riversport	885 River Rd.	Confluence	800-216-6991	Yes
GAP 72	Wilderness Voyageurs	PA381, 130 Garrett St	Ohiopyle	800-272-4141	Yes
GAP 72	Lrl Highlands Rvr Tours	Sherman St	Ohiopyle	800-472-3846	Yes
GAP 72	White Water Adv	Negley St	Ohiopyle	724-329-8850	Yes
GAP 72	Ohiopyle Rec Rentals	PA381, Commercial St	Ohiopyle	800-723-8669	Yes
GAP 72	Ohiopyle Trading Post	Negley St	Ohiopyle	724-329-1450	Yes
GAP 88	Bikes Unlimited	503 W. Crawford Av	Connellsville	724-628-2453	Yes
GAP 94	Youghiogheny Rentals	112 Railroad St	Dawson	724-529-2552	Yes
GAP 110	Cedar Creek Station	Cedar Creek Park	Belle Vernon	724-872-5586	Yes
GAP 114	West Newton Bikes	106 W Main St	W Newton	724-872-2185	Yes
GAP 126	River City Junction	242 Sandy Dr	Greenock	412-754-0976	Yes
GAP 128	Boston Shoppes	1903 Donner St	Boston	412-751-6695	Yes
GAP 128	Trailside Treasures	1910 Donner St	Boston	412-896-6015	Yes
GAP 132	Burke Lee's	2422 St David Dr	McKeesport	412-754-1490	Yes
TRHT	Golden Triangle Bike	Beside trail at 1st Ave	Pittsburgh	412-600-0675	Yes
TRHT	REI, Southside Works	1 block from trail	Pittsburgh	412-488-9410	No
In Pgh	Biketek Pittsburgh	5839 Forbes Ave	Pittsburgh	412-521-6448	Yes
In Pgh	Gatto Cycling & Fitness	7501 Penn Ave	Pittsburgh	412-731-9200	Yes
In Pgh	Trek Bicycles	5956 Penn Circle S	Pittsburgh	412-362-8735	

Restaurants and Grocery Stores

You need to eat along the trail. In urban areas there's no shortage of food. For example, in Georgetown (C&O 1) you can hardly throw a tire pump without hitting a restaurant. Here you don't need our help to find food. There are also restaurants near most indoor lodging. On some stretches, though, food is hard to find, even a convenience store has groceries, and a pizza shop counts as a restaurant. Restaurants and groceries come and go, but it's useful to know which towns are likely to have something that will keep you from starving.

Trail, MP	Town	*Restaurant*	*Grocery*	*Snacks*
C&O 1	Georgetown	Yes	Yes	Yes
C&O 3	Fletcher's Boat House	Bethesda (4 mi)	Bethesda (4 mi)	Yes
C&O 15	Great Falls	No	No	Yes
C&O 35	Whites Ferry	Leesburg (5 mi)	Leesburg (5 mi)	Yes
C&O 48	Point of Rocks	No	Yes	Yes
C&O 55	Brunswick	Yes	No	No
C&O 60	Sandy Hook / Harpers Ferry	Yes	No	Yes
C&O 73	Sharpsburg / Shepherdstown	Yes	Yes	Yes
C&O 100	Williamsport	Yes	Yes	Yes
C&O 124	Hancock	Yes	Yes	Yes
C&O 141	Little Orleans	Yes	Yes	Yes
C&O 156	Paw Paw	Yes	Yes	Yes
C&O 167	Oldtown	No	Yes	Yes
C&O 185	Cumberland	Yes	Yes	Yes
GAP 15	Frostburg	Yes	Yes	Yes
GAP 32	Meyersdale	Yes	Yes	Yes
GAP 36	Garrett	No	No	Yes
GAP 43	Rockwood	Yes	Yes	Yes
GAP 62	Confluence	Yes	Yes	Yes
GAP 72	Ohiopyle	Yes	Yes	Yes
GAP 88	Connellsville	Yes	Yes	Yes
GAP 92	Adelaide	No	No	Yes
GAP 94	Dawson	Yes	No	Across river
GAP 101	Layton	No	No	Across river
GAP 110	Cedar Creek Park	No	No	Yes
GAP 114	West Newton	Yes	Yes	Yes
GAP 117	Sutersville	Yes	No	Yes
GAP 120	Buena Vista	No	Yes	Yes
GAP 128	Boston	Yes	Yes	Yes
GAP 132	McKeesport	Yes	Yes	Yes
TRHT	Hazelwood	Yes	Yes	Yes
TRHT	Pittsburgh	Yes	Yes	Yes

Camping

This is a great camping trip because of the "hiker-biker" campsites along the C&O canal and the primitive camping at several points along the GAP. These trailside sites offer primitive camping (pump, chemical toilet, picnic table) shared with other hikers and bikers. They are located about every 5 to 10 miles from Swains Lock (C&O 16.7) to Cumberland (C&O 184.5) and at a few locations on the GAP. Water is from wells; at the Hiker-Biker sites, if the weekly test is suspect the NPS removes the pump handle, so carry plenty of water. These campsites, marked "primitive, no cars" in the table, are not accessible by car. Do not plan to use them unless you're carrying all your camping gear on your bikes. If you have more than 6-8 people or 4 tents in your party, don't count on using C&O Hiker-Bikers.

There are also car-accessible sites. The C&O canal offers primitive drive-in and walk-in sites (some without water). In addition to the C&O sites, there are a number of public and commercial campgrounds near the trail. Get directions for biking *from the trail* to the campground when you make reservations.

Our focus is on self-supported camping; these campgrounds are within easy biking distance of the trail (or the winter Savage Tunnel detour). Some are seasonal, so check availability. We are not personally familiar with most of the campgrounds. We present this information as a service, not a review or recommendation.

Trail, MP	Name	Dist From Tr	Type	Phone
C&O 11.5	Marsden Tract Group Camp	Beside trail	Primitive	301-767-3731
C&O 16.6	Swains Lock Hiker-Biker	Beside trail	Primitive, no cars	301-739-4200
C&O 26.0	Horsepen Branch Hiker-Biker	Beside trail	Primitive, no cars	301-739-4200
C&O 30.5	Chisel Branch Hiker-Biker	Beside trail	Primitive, no cars	301-739-4200
C&O 34.4	Turtle Run Hiker-Biker	Beside trail	Primitive, no cars	301-739-4200
C&O 38.2	Marble Quarry Hiker-Biker	Beside trail	Primitive, no cars	301-739-4200
C&O 42.4	Indian Flats Hiker-Biker	Beside trail	Primitive, no cars	301-739-4200
C&O 47.6	Calico Rocks Hiker-Biker	Beside trail	Primitive, no cars	301-739-4200
C&O 50.3	Bald Eagle Island Hiker-Biker	Beside trail	Primitive, no cars	301-739-4200
C&O 54.0	Brunswick Family Campground	Beside trail	Public developed	301-834-8050
C&O 59.6	Harpers Ferry Hostel (uphill)	0.3 mi SE	Tents at hostel	301-834-7652
C&O 62.9	Huckleberry Hill Hiker-Biker	Beside trail	Primitive, no cars	301-739-4200
C&O 69.4	Antietam Walk-in Camp	Beside trail	NPS primitive	301-739-4200
C&O 75.3	Killiansburg Cave Hiker-Biker	Beside trail	Primitive, no cars	301-739-4200
C&O 79.9	Horseshoe Bend Hiker-Biker	Beside trail	Primitive, no cars	301-739-4200
C&O 82.5	Big Woods Hiker-Biker	Beside trail	Primitive, no cars	301-739-4200
C&O 88.1	McMahon's Mill Campground	On detour	Commercial	301-223-8778
C&O 90.9	Opequon Junction Hiker-Biker	Beside trail	Primitive, no cars	301-739-4200
C&O 95.2	Cumberland Valley Hiker-Biker	Beside trail	Primitive, no cars	301-739-4200
C&O 99.4	Yogi Bear Jellystone Ground	3 mi SE	Commercial	800-421-7116

C&O 99.4	KOA Snug Harbor	2.5 mi NE	Commercial	301-223-7571
C&O 101.3	Jordan Junction Hiker-Biker	Beside trail	Primitive, no cars	301-739-4200
C&O 110.0	North Mountain Hiker-Biker	Beside trail	Primitive, no cars	301-739-4200
C&O 110.4	McCoy's Ferry Drive-in Camp	0.1 mi	NPS primitive	301-739-4200
C&O 112.4	Ft Frederick State Park	0.25 mi W	Public developed	301-842-2155
C&O 116.0	Licking Creek Hiker-Biker	Beside trail	Primitive, no cars	301-739-4200
C&O 120.4	Little Pool Hiker-Biker	Beside trail	Primitive, no cars	301-739-4200
C&O 126.4	White Rock Hiker-Biker	Beside trail	Primitive, no cars	301-739-4200
C&O 129.2	Happy Hills Campground (steep)	1 mi N	Commercial	301-678-7760
C&O 129.8	Leopards Mill Hiker-Biker	Beside trail	Primitive, no cars	301-739-4200
C&O 133.6	Cacapon Junction Hiker-Biker	Beside trail	Primitive, no cars	301-739-4200
C&O 139.2	Indigo Neck Hiker-Biker	Beside trail	Primitive, no cars	301-739-4200
C&O 140.8	Little Orleans Campground	1.5 mi W	Commercial	301-478-2325
C&O 140.8	15 Mile Ck Drive-in & grp tent	Beside trail	NPS primitive	301-739-4200
C&O 144.5	Devils Alley Hiker-Biker	Beside trail	Primitive, no cars	301-739-4200
C&O 149.4	Stickpile Hill Hiker-Biker	Beside trail	Primitive, no cars	301-739-4200
C&O 154.1	Sorrel Ridge Hiker-Biker	Beside trail	Primitive, no cars	301-739-4200
C&O 156.2	Paw Paw Walk-in Camp	Beside trail	Primitive, no cars	301-739-4200
C&O 156.9	Purslane Run Hiker-Biker	Beside trail	Primitive, no cars	301-739-4200
C&O 162.1	Town Creek Hiker-Biker	Beside trail	Primitive, no cars	301-739-4200
C&O 164.8	Potomac Forks Hiker-Biker	Beside trail	Primitive, no cars	301-739-4200
C&O 169.2	Pigmans Ferry Hiker-Biker	Beside trail	Primitive, no cars	301-739-4200
C&O 173.3	Spring Gap Drive-in Camp	Beside trail	NPS primitive	301-739-4200
C&O 175.4	Iron Mountain Hiker-Biker	Beside trail	Primitive, no cars	301-739-4200
C&O 180.0	Evitts Creek Hiker-Biker (noise)	Beside trail	Primitive, no cars	301-739-4200
GAP 0	Cumberland YMCA (train noise)	1.1 Mile N	Commercial	301 777-9622
GAP 15	Trail Inn Campground	Up to F'bg	Commercial	301-689-6466
GAP 24	Mason-Dixon Campground	On detour	Commercial	814-634-5982
GAP 43	Husky Haven Campground	Beside trail	Commercial	814-926-2024
GAP 62	Outflow Camping @ Yough Dam	0.2 mi S	Hiker-biker area	814-395-3944
GAP 62	Paddler's Lane Camp	2 mi N	Commercial	814-395-9555
GAP 62	Suder's Family Campground	2 mi S	Commercial	814-926-5396
GAP 72	Ohiopyle State Pk (up big hill)	Above trail	Public developed	724-329-8591
GAP 92	Rivers Edge Campground	Beside trail	Commercial	724-628-4880
GAP 100	Round Bottom Hiker Biker	Beside trail	Primitive, no cars	724-872-5586
GAP 101	Hazelbaker's Campground	1 mi X river	Comm, primitive	724-736-8155
GAP 110	Cedar Creek Hiker Biker	Beside trail	Primitive	724-872-5586
GAP 122	Dravo's Landing Camping	0.1 mi	Primitive, no cars	724-872-5586

Organized Boy and Girl Scout groups (only) may get permits to camp in town parks at Williamsport MD (C&O 100, call 301-223-7711) and Hancock MD (C&O 124, call 301-678-5622). Organized groups sponsored by nonprofit organizations may get permits to camp at the Marsden Tract (C&O 11.6, call 301-767-3731) and at Cedar Creek Park (GAP 110, call 724-830-3950). Group camping at Round Bottom (GAP 100) and Dravo's Landing (GAP 122) requires permit (free, call 724-872-5586).

Indoor Lodging

These are the B&Bs, hotels, motels and hostels that we know of near the trails. You're probably riding this trail to avoid riding in traffic, so we identify lodging as close to the trail as possible. Unfortunately, there's a 50-mile stretch northwest of Washington DC where almost all of the lodging is 5 miles off the trail, much of that distance in traffic. Be careful, or camp instead.

We are not personally familiar with most of the establishments. We present this information as a service; it is not a review or recommendation. When you make your reservations, ask for detailed directions for biking from the trail (not for driving directions from the highway). For a current list of lodging and other trailside services, check the ATA web site at http://www.ATATrail.org/.

Reminder: hotel and pay phones may have large long-distance surcharges. Remember to dial your long-distance service when you place calls from points along the trails.

Washington DC, Georgetown Area

We include only hotels within a few blocks of the C&O Towpath (either in Georgetown or near Rock Creek Park), plus the vastly less expensive DC Hostel. We include the Hostel with some qualms, because they no longer allow you to store bikes inside the building. As an inexpensive alternative, we include the International Guest House despite it distance from the towpath.

C&O 1	3 blocks N	Wash. Monarch Hotel	2401 M St NW	877-222-2266
C&O 1	Backs on trail	The Latham	3000 M St NW	800-368-5922
C&O 1	Backs on trail	Melrose Hotel	2430 Pennsylvania NW	800-635-7673
C&O 1	Backs on trail	Georgetown Suites	1111 30th St NW	800-568-7025
C&O 1	1 block	G'twn Suites/Harbor Bldg	1000 29th St	800-568-7025
C&O 1	2 blocks N	Monticello Hotel	1075 Tom Jefferson NW	202-337-0900
C&O 1	2 blocks N	Washington Suites	2500 Pennsylvania NW	202-333-8060
C&O 1	3 blocks E	Four Seasons Hotel	2800 Pennsylvania NW	800-819-5053
C&O 1	4 blocks N	Georgetown Inn	1310 Wisconsin Av	888-587-2388
C&O 1	5 blocks E	River Inn	924 25th St NW	888-874-0100
C&O 1	6 blocks	Hotel Lombardy	2019 Penn'a Ave NW	800-424-5486
C&O 1	8 blocks E	St Gregory	2033 M St NW	800-829-5034
C&O 1	1-2 mi	Tabard Inn	1739 N St NW	202-785-1277
C&O 1	1-2 mi NE	Washington Int'l Hostel	1009 11th St NW	202-737-2333
C&O 1	2 mi	The Inn of Rosslyn	1601 Arlington Blvd	703-524-3400
C&O 1	4 mi N	International Guest House	14th & Kennedy, near Rock Creek Park	202-726-5808
C&O 1	3 miles	Adams Inn B&B	1746 Lanier PL NW	800-578-6807
C&O 2	3 blocks E	Key Bridge Marriott	1401 Lee Hwy (Arlington)	703-524-6400

Bethesda MD

At Fletcher's Boathouse, cross over to the paved Capital Crescent Trail and follow the trail for 4 miles into Bethesda.

C&O 3	4 mi on trail	Residence Inn Marriott	7335 Wisconsin Av	800-331-3131
C&O 3	4 mi on trail	Bethesda Court Hotel	7740 Wisconsin Av	800-874-0050
C&O 3	4 mi on trail	Hyatt Regency	One Bethesda Metro Ctr	800-233-1234
C&O 3	4 mi on trail	American Inn	8130 Wisconsin Av	800-323-7081
C&O 3	4 mi on trail	Holiday Inn	8120 Wisconsin Av	800-465-4329

Potomac MD

C&O 12.3	.5 mi (up)	Rockwood Manor Park	11001 MacArthur Blvd	301-299-5026

Leesburg VA

At Whites Ferry (C&O 35.5), take the ferry across the Potomac. On the VA side climb to US15. Turn left on US15 (heavy traffic, be careful), then stay on Bus US15. Continue to VA7 in Leesburg; most lodging is within a mile. W&OD parallels VA7 two blocks to the south. Make prior arrangements for shuttle service to Norris House Inn, Best Western, and Comfort Inn Suites.

C&O 35	5 mi S	Colonial Inn	19 S King St	703-777-5000
C&O 35	5 mi S	Norris House Inn	108 Loudoun St SW	800-644-1806
C&O 35	6 mi S	Days Inn	721 E Market St	703-777-6622
C&O 35	6 mi S	Comfort Inn Suites	80 Prosperity Av	703-669-1650
C&O 35	6 mi S	Best Western Leesburg	726 E Market	703-777-9400

Dickerson MD

Dickerson is the MD town nearest miles 35-45 of the towpath. Pleasant Springs between Barnesville and Boyds.

C&O 42	8 mi E	Pleasant Spring Farm B&B	16112 Barnesville Road	301-972-3452

Brunswick MD / Sandy Hook MD / Harpers Ferry WV

Brunswick is across the canal nearly under the VA17 high bridge. Georges Mill Farm B&B provides shuttle service from Brunswick.

C&O 55	2 mi E	Green Country Inn	620 Souder Rd	301-834-9151
C&O 55	5 mi S	Georges Mill Farm B&B	Lovettsville, VA	540-822-5224

Sandy Hook is across the canal on a path nearly under the US340 high bridge. Cross the tracks carefully. Trains are reported to be fast and quiet.

C&O 58	1 mi uphill	Harpers Ferry Hostel	19123 Sandy Hook Rd	301-834-7652
C&O 59.5	1+ mi uphill	Hillside Motel	19105 Keep Tryst Rd	301-834-8144

Harpers Ferry: Climb stairs beside the trail, cross Potomac River on pedestrian bridge. Think twice before planning to carry loaded bikes up these stairs; it will probably take two people or two trips.

C&O 60.5	About a mile	Between the Rivers B&B	500 E Ridge St	304-535-2768

C&O 60.5	About a mile	Fillmore St B&B	630 Fillmore St	304-535-2619
C&O 60.5	About a mile	Harpers Ferry Guesthouse	800 Washington St	304-535-6955
C&O 60.5	About a mile	Jackson Rose B&B	1167 Washington St	304-535-1528
C&O 60.5	About a mile	Angler's Inn	867 Washington St	304-535-1239
C&O 60.5	About a mile	Last Resort	280 Clay St	304-535-2812
C&O 60.5	1 mile, up, up	Hilltop House	400 E Ridge St	304-535-2132
C&O 60.5	Over a mile	Comfort Inn	Shenandoah St & US340	304-535-6391

Shepherdstown WV / Sharpsburg MD

Shepherdstown: Just after Lock 38 cross the canal and take the new ramp under the bridge uphill to the western side of MD34. Take MD34 (becomes WV480, then Duke St) to cross Potomac River on the high bridge. B&Bs are within a mile.

C&O 73	1/2 mi SW	Bavarian Inn	Rt 480	304-876-2551
C&O 73	1 mi SW	Mecklenburg Inn	128 E German St	304-876-2126
C&O 73	1 mi SW	Thomas Shepherd Inn	300 W German St	888-889-8952
C&O 73	1 mi SW	Days Inn	2001 Maddex Sq Dr	304-876-3160
C&O 73	1 mi SW	Clarion Hotel & Suites	17 Lowe Dr	304-876-7000

Sharpsburg: At Snyder's Landing take Snyder's Landing Rd to Sharpsburg. Alternate: At Lock 38 (C&O 73) take the new ramp under the bridge uphill to the eastern side of MD34. Take MD34 away from the river for 3.5 miles in traffic; we have reports that the shoulder is decent most of the way.

C&O 77	2 mi E	Inn At Antietam	220 W Main St	301-432-6601
C&O 77	2 mi E	Jacob Rohrbach Inn	138 Main St	877-839-4242
C&O 77	2.5 mi E	Piper House	Antietam Battlefield	301-797-1862
C&O 77	7 mi E	Antietam Overlook Farm	Keedysville	301-432-4200

Williamsport MD

C&O 94	On detour	Wolfs End B&B	14940 Falling Water Rd	301-223-6888
C&O 99.4	1 mi N	Red Roof Inn	310 E Potomac St	301-582-3500

Hancock MD

C&O 123	2 blocks N	Hancock Truck Stop	434 E Main St	301-678-7111
C&O 124	Across canal	C&O Bicycle Bunkhouse	9 S Pennsylvania Av	301-678-6665
C&O 124	1/2 mile	1828 Trail Inn	10 West Main St	301-678-7227
C&O 124	3/4 mi NW	Super 8	118 Limestone Rd	301-678-6101
C&O 124	1 mi W	America's Best Value	2 Blue Hill	301-678-6108

Little Orleans MD

Town Hill is seven miles up a hill, but they'll come get you; call from Bill's in Little Orleans. Buck Valley Ranch offers free shuttle to and from towpath.

C&O 141	1/2 mi	Little Orleans Lodge	12814 Appel Rd	301-478-2102
C&O 141	Pickup	Town Hill Hotel	National Pike NE	877-696-2794
C&O 141	Pickup	Buck Valley Ranch	1344 Negro Mtn. Rd.	800-294-3759

Paw Paw WV

Take short hill down to a parking lot. Exit to MD51 (becomes WV9), turn left, cross bridge.

C&O 156	3/4 mi S	Grandma's Country Inn	103 Winchester St	800-580-4225
C&O 156	3/4 mi S	Heritage Trail B&B	107 Winchester St	304-947-7055

Cumberland MD

Cumberland and LaVale have many motels, but only two are near the trail. In addition, the Best Western and Rocky Gap will pick you up; ask them in advance.

C&O 185	5 blocks E	Holiday Inn	100 S George St	877-426-4672
C&O 185	8 blocks W	Inn At Walnut Bottom	120 Greene St	800-286-9718
C&O 185	9 blocks W	Bruce House Inn	210 Fayette St	866-777-8181
C&O 185	10 blocks E	The Inn on Decatur	108 Decatur St	800-459-0510
C&O 185	Pickup	Braddock Best Western	1268 National Hwy	800-296-6006
C&O 185	Pickup	Rocky Gap Resort	16701 Lakeview Rd	301-784-8400

Frostburg MD

From the trail head uphill on the switch backs to the railroad station. At the station turn left and continue uphill to the town. For Castle, exit trail at Paddy Baker Rd.

GAP 12	1 mi down	Castle Bed & Breakfast	15925 Mt Savage Rd	301-264-4645
GAP 15	4 blocks	Failinger's Hotel Gunter	11 W Main St	301-689-6511
GAP 15	0.3 mi E	Frostburg Inn	147 E Main St	301-689-3831
GAP 15	0.1 mi	Trail Inn & Café	20 Depot St.	301-689-6466
GAP 15	1 mi W	Charlie's Motel	220 W Main St	888-230-9053
GAP 15	1.5 mi S	Frostburg St U dorms	Call for instructions	301-687-4020
GAP 15	2 mi SE	Day's Inn	11100 MD 36	301-689-2050
GAP 15	2 mi SE	Hampton Inn	11200 MD 36	301-689-1998

Meyersdale PA

GAP 32	0.2 mi	Levi Deal Mansion	301 Meyers Avenue	443-812-6317
GAP 32	0.3 mi	Main Street Inn	322 Main St	814-634-8236
GAP 32	0.4 mi	Burgess' House	219 North St.	814-662-2436
GAP 32	0.4 mi	Maple City Loft	130 Center St.	814-634-5121
GAP 32	0.4 mi	Allegheny Trail Hostel	215 Main St , 814-634-5743	814-634-8478 814-634-9100
GAP 32	0.4 mi	Yoder's Motel	106 Myers Ave	814-634-8791

Rockwood PA

The B&Bs marked "pickup" are 5-12 miles from the trail, with hills and traffic. They will pick you up at the trailhead by prior arrangement.

GAP 43	At trailhead	Rockwood Trail House	131 Rockdale Rd	814-926-4778
GAP 43	At trailhead	Husky Haven Guesthouse	440 Water St	814-926-2024
GAP 43	At trailhead	Gingerbread House B&B	156 Rockdale Road	814-926-2542

GAP 43	Pickup	Laurel Echo Farm	174 Cross Rd	814-926-2760
GAP 43	Pickup	Country Dreams B&B	882 Chippewa Rd	814-926-4774
GAP 43	Pickup	Log Haven B&B	1322 Trent Rd	814-352-8971
GAP 43	Pickup	Trent House B&B	2008 Copper Kettle	888-352-8221
GAP 43	Pickup	Glades Pike Inn	2684 Glades Pike	800-762-5942

Markleton PA

Up the hill; call and they'll pick you up

GAP 50	Pickup	Four Seasons Guest Ranch	450 Porter Rd	814-926-3572

Harnedsville PA

GAP 59	.4 mi	Hanna House B&B	1790 Listonburg Rd	814-395-9466
GAP 59	1 mi.	Stepping Stone Farm	140 Stepping Stone Ln	814-395-9988

Confluence PA

Jacobs, Yough, and Sterner Sts are in the triangle of land between the Youghiogheny and Casselman Rivers.

GAP 62	4 block	That Dam Yough House	615 Jacobs St	800-278-7287
GAP 62	4 blocks	River's Edge Cafe & B&B	203 Yough St	814-395-5059
GAP 62	5 blocks	Parker House	213 Yough St	814-395-9616
GAP 62	6 blocks	The House at Confluence	415 Sterner St	724-468-0058
GAP 62	3 blocks	Confluence House B&B	522 Oden St	814-352-8151
GAP 62	3 blocks	Colonial House B&B	639 Oden St	814-395-3869
GAP 62	8 blocks	Dodds hotel	460 Latrobe Ave	814-395-3889
GAP 62	2 mi	River Rest B&B	194 Weyand Ave	814-395-3969
GAP 62	2 mi	Paddler's Lane B&B	255 Paddler's Lane	800-777-6061

Ohiopyle PA

Quiet House B&B is 8 hilly miles away; they will pick you up.

GAP 72	Beside trail	Falls Market and Inn	69 Main St	724-329-4973
GAP 72	2 blocks	Yough Plaza Motel	28 Sherman St	800-992-7238
GAP 72	3 blocks	Ohiopyle Guest House	4 Sherman St.	800-644-6795
GAP 72	4 blocks	Laurel Highlands River Tours B&B	Sherman St	724-329-8531
GAP 72	5 blocks	Ohiopyle Lodge	138 Grant St	800-419-7599
GAP 72	8 blocks	Hummingbird Guest Nest	107 Blaine St	724-329-5301
GAP 72	Pickup	Quiet House B&B	667 Elliotsville Rd	724-329-4606

Connellsville PA

GAP 88	1 mi S, traffic	Melody Motor Lodge	Rt 119 S	724-628-9600

Dawson PA

GAP 94	3 mi, 500' up	Linden Hall Corp	Up Stone Bridge Trail	724-529-7543

Layton PA

GAP 101	1.5 mi, up	Inn at Lenora's	301 Liberty St	724-736-2509

Smithton PA

At the Smithton parking lot (YRTN 39.3), take the ramp out of the parking lot, turn right onto PA981, and climb a mile or two to the motels. Fairway Inn will pick you up if you call. Another alternative is to go on to Cedar Creek Park, climb out in the park, and make your way along the highway to the interchange

GAP 108	1.5-2 mi W	Fairway Inn	PA981 nr PA51 & I70	724-929-6677
GAP 108	1.5-2 mi W	Sleeper Inn	at PA51 near I70	724-929-4501
GAP 108	1.5-2 mi W	Holiday Inn	Finley Rd (PA51 nr I70)	724-929-4600
GAP 108	1.5-2 mi W	Relax Inn	833 Finley Rd	724-929-6770

West Newton PA

GAP 114	3 blocks	Bright Morning B&B	127 Jefferson Ct	724-872-0792
GAP 114	5 blocks W	Scarsdale Cottage Inn	208 Allison St	724-872-2121

Buena Vista PA

GAP 120	1 mile S (up)	John Butler House B&B	800 Rock Run Rd	412-751-6670

Boston PA

GAP 128	4 blocks	Yough Shore Inn	1403 Boston Hollow Rd	412-754-0440

Pittsburgh PA

Pittsburgh has many hotels. The closest to MP 0 at The Point is the Hilton. The closest to the downtown end of Eliza Furnace Trail is the Omni William Penn. The Westin is near the Amtrak station. The Holiday Inn Select, Wyndham Garden, and Hampton are in Oakland, near the north end of the Junction Hollow extension of the Eliza Furnace Trail. Appletree B&B is also near the north end of the Junction Hollow Trail and will shuttle bikers to McKeesport by prior arrangement. Holiday Inn Express and Morning Glory are in SouthSide near the trail.

SVT	1 block	Courtyard	401 W Waterfront Dr	412-462-7301
TRHT	Near MP 0	Hilton Pittsburgh Towers	600 Commonwealth	412-391-4600
TRHT	6 blocks N	Omni William Penn	530 William Penn Place	412-281-7100
TRHT	8 blocks N	Westin Convention Center	1000 Penn Av	412-281-3700
TRHT	1 miN	Holiday Inn Sel - Univ Ctr	100 Lytton Av	412-682-6200
TRHT	1 mi N	Wyndham Garden Hotel	3454 Forbes Ave	412-683-2040
TRHT	1 mi N	Hampton Inn	315 Hamlet St	412-681-1000
TRHT	2 mi NE	Appletree B&B	703 S Negley Ave	412-661-0631
TRHT	2 blocks	Holiday Inn Express	20 S 10th St	412-488-1130
TRHT	0.5 mi S	Morning Glory Inn	2119 Sara St	412-431-1707
TRHT	11 blocks	Inn of Mexican War Sts	604 W North Ave	412-231-6544

Milepost Conversion and Points of Interest

In 2006 the Great Allegheny Passage received a unified mileage system with a single set of mileposts that starts in Cumberland and counts toward Pittsburgh. Previously the trails were numbered individually, sometimes in different directions. The new mileposts may be adjusted a little when the trail is complete, but they're accurate enough for planning purposes. This table shows the locations of places along the trail, the conversion between the new and old mileposts, and the distance from Washington DC.

The new mileage system measures distances through the Pinkerton Tunnel, which is currently closed. An interim trail runs around the Pinkerton Neck; the interim trail is about a mile longer than the final trail will be. As a result, the trail mileage between Markleton and Ft Hill is about a mile longer than the mileposts suggest.

Location	GAP Milepost	Old Milepost	Distance from DC
Cumberland	0		185
	1		186
National Road Bridge	2		187
	3		188
	4		189
	5		190
Brush Tunnel	6		191
	7		192
	8		193
Woodcock Hollow	9		194
	10		195
	11		196
	12		197
	13		198
Switch Number 9	14		199
Frostburg	15		200
	16		201
	17		202
Borden Tunnel	18		203
	19		204
	20		205
Mason-Dixon Line	21		206
Big Savage Tunnel	22		207
	23		208
Continental Divide	24		209
Deal	25		210
	26		211
	27		212
Sand Patch	28		213

Location	GAP Milepost	Old Milepost	Distance from DC
	29		214
Keystone Viaduct,	30		215
	31		216
Meyersdale	32	AHTPa 11	217
Salisbury Viaduct	33	AHTPa 12	218
	34	AHTPa 13	219
	35	AHTPa 14	220
Garrett	36	AHTPa 15	221
	37	AHTPa 16	222
	38	AHTPa 17	223
	39	AHTPa 18	224
	40	AHTPa 19	225
	41	AHTPa 20	226
	42	AHTPa 21	227
Rockwood	43	AHTPa 22	228
	44	AHTPa 23	229
	45	AHTPa 24	230
	46	AHTPa 25	231
	47	AHTPa 26	232
	48	AHTPa 27	233
	49	AHTPa 28	234
Markleton	50	AHTPa 29	235
	51	AHTPa 30	236
Pinkerton Tunnel	52	AHTPa 31	237
	detour	detour	238
	53	AHTPa 32	239
Ft Hill	54	AHTPa 33	240
	55	AHTPa34	241
	56	AHTPa 35	242

Location	GAP Milepost	Old Milepost	Distance from DC
	57	AHTPa 36	243
	58	AHTPa 37	244
Harnedsville	59	AHTPa 38	245
	60	AHTPa 39	246
Confluence	61	AHTPa 40	247
Confluence @ Yough	62	AHTPa 41	248
Ramcat Hollow	63	YRTS 1	249
	64	YRTS 2	250
	65	YRTS 3	251
	66	YRTS 4	252
	67	YRTS 5	253
	68	YRTS 6	254
	69	YRTS 7	255
	70	YRTS 8	256
	71	YRTS 9	257
Ohiopyle	72	YRTS 10	258
	73	YRTS 11	259
	74	YRTS 12	260
	75	YRTS 13	261
	76	YRTS 14	262
	77	YRTS 15	263
	78	YRTS 16	264
Bruner Run, Overlook	79	YRTS 17	265
	80	YRTS 18	266
Camp Carmel	81	YRTS 19	267
	82	YRTS 20	268
	83	YRTS 21	269
	84	YRTS 22	270
	85	YRTS 23	271
Wheeler Bottom	86	YRTS 24	272
	87	YRTS 25	273
Connellsville	88	YRTS 26	274
Connellsville	89	YRTN 58	275
	90	YRTN 57	276
	91	YRTN 56	277
Adelaide	92	YRTN 55	278
	93	YRTN 54	279
Dawson/Dickerson	94	YRTN 53	280
	95	YRTN 52	281
	96	YRTN 51	282
	97	YRTN 50	283
	98	YRTN 49	284
	99	YRTN 48	285
Round Bottom	100	YRTN 47	286
Layton	101	YRTN 46	287
	102	YRTN 45	288
	103	YRTN 44	289

Location	GAP Milepost	Old Milepost	Distance from DC
Whitsett	104	YRTN 43	290
	105	YRTN 42	291
	106	YRTN 41	292
Van Meter	107	YRTN 40	293
Smithton	108	YRTN 39	294
	109	YRTN 38	295
Cedar Creek Park	110	YRTN 37	296
	111	YRTN 36	297
Buddtown	112	YRTN 35	298
West Newton	113	YRTN 34	299
West Newton	114	YRTN 33	300
Collinsburg	115	YRTN 32	301
Smithdale	116	YRTN 31	302
Sutersville	117	YRTN 30	303
Blythedale	118	YRTN 29	304
Industry	119	YRTN 28	305
Buena Vista	120	YRTN 27	306
	121	YRTN 26	307
Dravo Cemetery	122	YRTN 25	308
	123	YRTN 24	309
	124	YRTN 23	310
	125	YRTN 22	311
Greenock	126	YRTN 21	312
	127	YRTN 20	313
Boston	128	YRTN 19	314
Deadman's Hollow	129	YRTN 18	315
Durabond Overlook	130	YRTN 17	316
	131	YRTN 16	317
McKeesport	132	YRTN 15	318
(unbuilt)	133		319
(unbuilt)	134		320
(unbuilt)	135		321
(unbuilt)	136		322
(unbuilt)	137		323
(unbuilt)	138		324
(unbuilt)	139		325
Homestead	140		326
(unbuilt)	141		327
Waterfront	142		328
(unbuilt)	143		329
	144		330
	145		331
Eliza Trail	146		332
	147		333
	148		334
Pittsburgh	149		335

Mileage Chart

This chart gives the distances between towns along the Great Allegheny Passage between Pittsburgh PA and Washington DC. It covers only the direct route; a future edition will include distances along the Montour Trail to Pittsburgh Airport.

***Pittsburgh** GAP 149*

***Homestead** GAP 140 (GAP 133-143 still incomplete in 2007)*	9													
***McKeesport** GAP 132*	17	8												
***Boston** GAP 128*	21	12	4											
***Sutersville** GAP 117*	32	23	15	11										
***West Newton** GAP 114*	36	27	19	15	4									
***Smithton** GAP 108*	41	32	24	20	9	5								
***Dawson** GAP 94*	55	46	38	34	23	19	14							
***Connellsville** GAP 88*	60	51	43	39	28	24	19	5						
***Ohiopyle** GAP 72*	77	68	60	56	45	41	36	22	17					
***Confluence** GAP 62 Note #1*	88	79	71	67	56	52	47	33	28	11				
***Rockwood** GAP 43*	107	98	90	86	75	71	66	52	47	30	19			
***Meyersdale** GAP*	118	109	101	97	86	82	77	63	58	41	30	11		
MD/PA line	129	120	112	108	97	93	88	74	69	52	41	22	11	
	135	126	118	114	103	99	94	80	75	58	47	28	17	6
	150	141	133	129	118	114	109	95	90	73	62	43	32	21
	179	170	162	158	147	143	138	124	119	102	91	72	61	50
	194	185	177	173	162	158	153	139	134	117	106	87	76	65
	211	202	194	190	179	175	170	156	151	134	123	104	93	82
	235	226	218	214	203	199	194	180	175	158	147	128	117	106
	262	253	245	241	230	226	221	207	202	185	174	155	144	133
	274	265	257	253	242	238	233	219	214	197	186	167	156	145
	287	278	270	266	255	251	246	232	227	210	199	180	169	158
	300	291	283	279	268	264	259	245	240	223	212	193	182	171
	321	312	304	300	289	285	280	266	261	244	233	214	203	192
	335	326	318	314	303	299	294	280	275	258	247	228	217	206

Mileage Chart

The chart shows distances along the trail, rounded to the nearest mile. Distances along road detours may differ substantially. You will ride a few miles more off the trail to buy supplies or go to and from your motel or B&B.

To find the distance for your trip:

Select starting and ending points for trip

Read down from northern end and left from southern end

Example: Between Confluence and Hancock is 123 trail miles

Note #1: GAP mileage from Rockwood to Confluence is measured through Pinkerton tunnel so GAP mileposts suggest shorter than actual trail distances.

Frostburg *GAP 15*											
15	***Cumberland*** *GAP 0*										
44	29	***Paw Paw*** *C&O 156*									
59	44	15	***Little Orleans*** *C&O 141*								
76	61	32	17	***Hancock*** *C&O 124*							
100	85	56	41	24	***Williamsport*** *C&O 100*						
127	112	83	68	51	27	***Shepherdstown*** *C&O 73*					
139	124	95	80	63	39	12	***Harpers Ferry*** *C&O 61*				
152	137	108	93	76	52	25	13	***Point of Rocks*** *C&O 48*			
165	150	121	106	89	65	38	26	13	***Whites Ferry*** *C&O 35*		
186	171	142	127	110	86	59	47	34	21	***Great Falls*** *C&O 14*	
200	185	156	141	124	100	73	61	48	35	14	***Washington***

Trail Sections and Support Groups

Great Allegheny Passage Allegheny Trail Alliance P.O. Box 501 Latrobe, PA 15650 888-ATA-BIKE ATAmail@ATAtrail.org www.ATATrail.org	**C&O Canal National Historic Park** C&O Canal National Historic Park 1850 Dual Highway, Suite 100 Hagerstown, MD 21740-6620 301-739-4200 www.nps.gov/choh
Allegany County, MD Allegheny Highlands Trails Maryland PO Box 28 Cumberland MD 21502 www.AHTMTrail.org	**Somerset County, PA** Somerset County Rails to Trails Assn PO Box 413 Somerset PA 15501 814-445-1573 info@bikesomersetcountypa.com www.bikesomersetcountypa.com
Youghiogheny River Trail South Friends of Ohiopyle State Park Ohiopyle State Park PO Box 105 Ohiopyle PA 15470-0105 724-329-8591 ohiopylesp@state.pa.us www.dcnr.state.pa.us/stateparks/parks/ohio.htm	**Youghiogheny River Trail North** Regional Trail Corporation PO Box 95, 111 W Main St West Newton PA 15089 724-872-5586 youghrivertrail@verizon.net www.youghrivertrail.com
Steel Valley Trail Steel Valley Trail Council PO Box 318 Homestead PA 15120 Info@steelvalleytrail.org www.steelvalleytrail.org	**Three Rivers Heritage Trail** Friends of the Riverfront 33 Terminal Way Pittsburgh PA 15219 412-488-0212 friends@friendsoftheriverfront.org www.friendsoftheriverfront.org
Montour Trail Montour Trail Council PO Box 11866 Pittsburgh PA 15228-0866 412-257-0311 info@montourtrail.org www.montourtrail.org	

Most trails are developed and maintained by volunteers and member contributions. When you find trails you enjoy, please support them.